A Pictorial Survey of
RAILWAY SIGNALLING

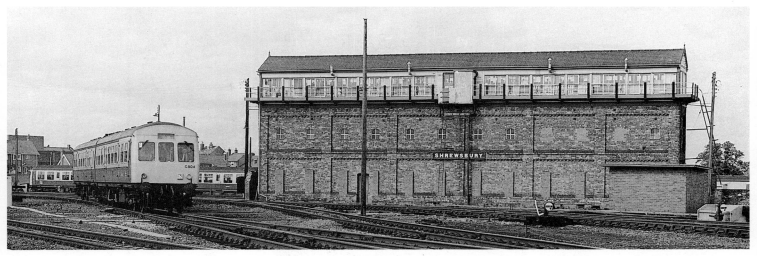

The impressive, and well known, Severn Bridge Junction signal box at Shrewsbury. A Class 101 dmu forms the 15.50 Shrewsbury to Swansea working on 22nd August 1985.

Class 25/2 No. 25213 heads the Severn Tunnel Junction–Mossend Yard Speedlink service at Moreton-on-Lugg on 28th May 1985.

A PICTORIAL SURVEY OF

RAILWAY SIGNALLING

D ALLEN & C J WOOLSTENHOLMES

Oxford Publishing·Co.

British Library Cataloguing in Publication Data

Allen, D.H.
    Railway Signalling.
    1. Great Britain. Railways. Signalling equipment.
    1. Title. II. Woolstenholmes, C.J.
    625.1650941
ISBN 0 86093 453 5

Library of Congress catalog card number
91-71118

Editor: Peter Nicholson.
Page layout: Jill Moulton.

Oxford Publishing Co. is part of the
Haynes Publishing Group
Sparkford, Near Yeovil, Somerset. BA22 7JJ

Haynes Publications Inc.
861 Lawrence Drive, Newbury Park, California 91320, USA.

Printed by: J.H. Haynes & Co. Ltd
Typeset in 9/10pt Times Roman.

Dedication

To the train crews, signalmen and S. & T. staff of British Rail and their predecessors.

Acknowledgements

We are grateful to those officers of BR who have afforded us facilities to visit signal boxes during the last decade. Our thanks are due also to the following friends and members of the Signalling Record Society – all experts in their own particular areas of study – who have kindly given help: Michael Back, Bruce Bennett, David Collins, Martin Elms, Richard Foster, Ed Nicoll, Ralph Potter, Clive Robey, John Talbot and Garth Tilt.
    All photographs are by David Allen.

The Signalling Record Society

The Signalling Record Society was founded in 1969 and is the country's only society specialising in the study of railway signalling and operation in the British Isles and overseas. If railway signalling interests you, why not discover more and for a prospectus of membership please write to: The Membership Secretaries, SRS, 18 Boston Avenue, Reading, Berkshire RG1 6JU.

Contents

Introduction

British railway traction, rolling stock and signalling have evolved beyond recognition since those early days of the 1840s, a century and a half ago, when primitive steam locomotives, stage-coach style carriages and railway traffic policemen were the state of the art. In the intervening years, significant advances were achieved, but it is perhaps only during the last decade that technical developments in mechanical and signal engineering have rivalled the progress of the 1930s and have been so rapid, innovative and far-reaching. For example, the five PSB schemes at Colchester, Doncaster, Leicester, Victoria/Three Bridges and Exeter/Westbury have seen the elimination of over 210 mechanical cabins, while Inverness RETB Signalling Centre is responsible for the control of 250 route miles of railway – the largest geographical area in Great Britain.

With the arrival of the concept of the Integrated Electronic Control Centre – a new breed of super-powerful computer-controlled signal box, combining the latest hi-tech developments of Solid State Interlocking and Automatic Route Setting, with high-resolution colour VDUs, (installations already commissioned at Liverpool Street, Marylebone, Yoker and York) – virtually anything is now possible in the realm of signal engineering and control. It seems almost certain that, by the millennium, British Rail will have achieved its objective of controlling the majority of InterCity, Regional Railways, Network SouthEast and Railfreight routes from the 75 or so signalling centres envisaged in the National Signalling Plan.

However, in compiling this overview of British Rail operating and signalling practice in the 1980s, it has been our aim to combine these elements within an attractive and varied context, in terms of traction, train services and the rural and industrial environment adjacent to the railway, and to explain them concisely and simply, for both the lay observer and the interested amateur. This has proved to be a challenging task. Compromises, therefore, have had to be made in the selection of photographs presented and some aspects, for instance the less photogenic and the more technical, which are outside the scope of this general volume, have deliberately been omitted. A departure from previous pictorial albums has been the subdivision of the majority of the captions into a general and signalling section. The signalling captions form a continuous narrative. When identified in the text, signals and points are given their correct BR nomenclature and number in the lever frame. The architectural classification of signal box types and the abbreviations are based on those found in *The Signal Box* (OPC). A new section dealing principally with the most used signalling and other general terms has been added. Although a number of standard texts on signalling have been consulted in the preparation of this survey, for a concise detailed treatise about BR signalling methods and systems/practices, the reader is referred to *British Railway Signalling,* (4th edition), Kichenside and Williams, Ian Allan, 1978, now unfortunately out of print.

Inevitably, by the time this book is published, certain changes in the BR infrastructure, of which the authors are aware, will have been implemented.

Abbreviations

Railways Companies:

BR	British Rail
BR(AR)	British Rail, Anglia Region (from 1.4.88)
BR(ER)	British Rail, Eastern Region (excluding BR(AR) from 1.4.1988)
BR(LMR)	British Rail, London Midland Region
BR(NER)	British Rail, North Eastern Region (1948-1966)
BR(ScR)	British Rail, Scottish Region
BR(SR)	British Rail, Southern Region
BR(WR)	British Rail, Western Region
BTC	British Transport Commission
CLC	Cheshire Lines Committee
CR	Caledonian Railway
GC	Great Central Railway
GE	Great Eastern Railway
GN	Great Northern Railway
GNoS	Great North of Scotland Railway
GSW	Glasgow & South Western Railway
GW	Great Western Railway
L&Y	Lancashire & Yorkshire Railway
LBSC	London, Brighton & South Coast Railway
LCD	London, Chatham & Dover Railway
LMS	London, Midland & Scottish Railway
LNER	London & North Eastern Railway
LNW	London & North Western Railway
LSW	London & South Western Railway
LT	London Transport
M&C	Maryport & Carlisle Railway
M&GN	Midland & Great Northern Joint Railway
MR	Midland Railway
MS&L	Manchester, Sheffield & Lincolnshire Railway
NB	North British Railway
NE	North Eastern Railway
NS	North Staffordshire Railway
SE	South Eastern Railway
SR	Southern Railway

Signalling Contractors:

EOD	Evans, O'Donnell
GRSCo	General Railway Signal Company
McK&H	McKenzie & Holland
RSCo	Railway Signal Company
S&F	Saxby & Farmer
SGE	Siemens & General Electric Railway Signal Company
STC	Standard Telephones & Cables
WB&SCo	Westinghouse Brake & Signal Company (1935-1980)

Signalling and General Terms:

AB	Absolute Block
AHB	Automatic Half Barriers
AOCL	Automatic Open Crossing (Locally monitored)
ARP	Air Raid Precautions
BTF	Brick to Floor
CCTV	Closed Circuit Television
dmu	Diesel multiple unit
demu	Diesel-electric multiple unit
ECML	East Coast Main Line
ECS	Empty Coaching Stock
EKT	Electric Key Token
emu	Electric multiple unit
GF	Ground Frame
HST	High Speed Train
IB	Intermediate Block
IECC	Integrated Electronic Control Centre
IFS	Individual Function Switch
MAS	Multiple Aspect Signalling
MCB	Manned Controlled Barriers
mgr	Merry-go-round
MoT	Ministry of Transport
MWL	Miniature Warning Lights
NRM	National Railway Museum
'N-X'	eNtrance-eXit
OC	Open Crossing
'OCS'	One Control Switch
OLE	Overhead Line Equipment
OTW	One Train Working
PB	Permissive Block
PSB	Panel Signal Box
PSR	Permanent Speed Restriction
RETB	Radio Electronic Token Block
S&T	Signal & Telecommunications
SLW	Single Line Working
SSI	Solid State Interlocking
TB	Tokenless Block
TCB	Track Circuit Block
TMO	Train Man Operated
TOPS	Total Operations Processing System
VDU	Visual Display Unit
WCML	West Coast Main Line

Reference Books:

GWS	*Great Western Signalling*, A. Vaughan (OPC)
LNERS	*LNER Constituent Signalling*, A.A. Maclean (OPC)
LNWRS	*LNWR Signalling*, R.D. Foster (OPC)
SB	*The Signal Box*, Signalling Study Group (OPC)
SS	*Southern Signals*, G.A. Pryer (OPC)

1 : Nostalgia

Plate 1

Approaching Taunton on the Down Relief line – most of which was lifted when power signalling was inaugurated – is the 07.30 Aberdeen to Penzance service on 6th July 1984. This line came into being in 1931 when the flyover to carry the Down Bristol line over the Up and Down London lines was constructed at Cogload. (The Down Relief was the extension of the Down Bristol line.) The locomotive, Class 50 No. 50049 *Defiance,* was experimentally converted for the Railfreight sector and renumbered No. 50149 in September 1987. No other examples were similarly treated and it was transferred to Departmental duties in January 1989. It regained its former number the following month and was allocated to Network SouthEast for work on Waterloo to Salisbury/Exeter services.

Our signalling survey begins on the GW with a glimpse of some 'gorgeous' gantries, alas now no more. These signals at the eastern exit from Taunton station used to control the Up Relief line (left) and the Up Main (right); the centre pair of signals read through the facing crossover below the fourth coach. The lower miniature arms were all calling-on signals (see Plates 23 and 24). The train has just passed signal No. 136 and is approaching on the Down Relief line. Control of the signalling in the Taunton area was transferred to Exeter PSB on 23rd March 1987.

Plate 2

Class 45/1 No. 45105 draws out of Taunton with the empty stock off the 16.15 service from Bristol Temple Meads on 6th July 1984. After propelling the stock through the station the train formed the 17.40 return working. This 'fill-in' turn, for the locomotive arriving on the 23.50 ex-Glasgow Central before leaving on the 21.24 return service, was diagrammed for a Class 47/4 but was frequently worked by a 'Peak'. The scheduled use of locomotives on these local services was due to cease in May 1988, but problems with Class 155 'Sprinters' led to frequent substitutions after this date. (On the right is part of the West Loop which – avoided the station to the south – and rejoined the mainline at Taunton East Junction. This deviation was truncated during resignalling and is now only used for access to the East Yard.)

In the good old days, this magnificent gantry at the west end of Taunton station used to carry no less than 22 arms, thought to be a record for a GW/BR(WR) gantry. The train is drawing forward under the authority of No. 6 Down Main shunt-ahead (bottom arm third doll from right). The roof of Taunton West cabin can be seen above the second coach. The cabin and semaphores were replaced by colour light signals controlled from a temporary panel in Taunton East box on 12th May 1986.

Plate 3
Since the summer of 1984, North West/West Country services have been worked by locomotives and HSTs. One such service, the 09.36 Liverpool Lime Street to Penzance, is seen approaching Newton Abbot on the Down Main on 9th August 1984. The locomotive, No. 47611, had recently been converted from Class 47/0 No. 47166 and was named *Thames* the following month. This name was formerly carried by Class 47/4 No. 47511, but was removed when the locomotive was converted for 'push-pull' operation on the Scottish Region. Since resignalling the Heathfield branch (left) remains but the tracks under the gantry (Up Through and Up Main [platform 4]) have been lifted and the former platform 3/4 (right) has been shortened and is no longer an island.

The remodelling and re-signalling of Newton Abbot station was completed in 1928, when this gantry at the east end originally with 11 signal arms, controlling the Up Through (left), Up Main and Up Relief lines, was erected (for official drawing, and detailed textual description, see *GWS*, Plate 55). Two new timber signal boxes, to GW Type 28, East (with 206 levers) and West (153 levers) [see *GWS* pages 139/140 for building costs], were constructed, together with Aller Junction and Dainton Tunnel cabins. Both Newton Abbot boxes were closed on 4th May 1987, when MAS controlled from Exeter PSB was commissioned.

Plate 4
Class 45/0 No. 45006 *Honourable Artillery Company* restarts the 09.21 Leeds to Penzance service out of Newton Abbot on 9th August 1984. Prior to 1975 this train was the "Cornishman", the title being lost when it was decreed that the "..... train had fallen short of the standards required by a named Inter-City service .... " (British Rail). Fortunately, the name was resurrected in 1986 when it was used on the 07.30 service from Aberdeen, and subsequently applied to various HST services originating on the East Coast. The original "Cornishman" commenced running in June 1890 and was the forerunner of the "Cornish Riviera Express". After being replaced by the latter in 1904 the name did not reappear until July 1935 when it was used as the official relief to the "Cornish Riviera". The first use by BR was in 1952 when the Wolverhampton Low Level to Penzance service – via Honeybourne – was so named.

That track rationalisation at the west end of Newton Abbot station has occurred can be deduced from the state of the gantry, with two posts (or dolls) each shorn of two signals. Spanning the Down Relief line (left) and Down Through (right), the gantry once carried twelve arms, all the lower ones being calling-on signals. Next to No. 2 Down Main Home signal (at proceed) is No. 16 Down Main to Down Relief signal. The centre pair of signals read Down Relief Home (lever 15) while the right-hand pair read Down Through to Down Main (arms removed) and Down Through Home (lever 19). Newton Abbot East box can be seen to the left of No. 19 signal doll.

Plate 5
7V80, the 05.35 Salisbury to Meldon Quarry ballast empties emerges from the morning mist on 10th August 1984 and approaches Exeter Central hauled by Class 33/1 No. 33101. (This train was routed via Westbury [reverse] and Castle Cary before gaining the former LSW West of England main line at Yeovil Junction.) Meldon produces a high quality granite ballast which supplies the bulk of the requirements of the BR(SR) and BR(WR).

This balanced bracket signal on the approach to Exeter Central station from Exmouth Junction read to the Down Through line (signal at clear), the Down Platform (centre arm) and the Down Bay Platform. The post was manufactured from redundant bullhead rails (see Plate 94) and the three dolls were lattice steel with ex-LSW cruciform finials, adopted as standard by the SR. Note the already-dug foundation for its replacement by a three-aspect colour light signal No. 310, with off-set subsidiary (see Plate 168), on 28th October 1984, when all the semaphore signals controlled from Exeter Central "A" box were abolished and colour lights introduced, under Stage 1 (Preliminary Works) of the Exeter Re-signalling programme.

Plate 6
Journey's end for the 11.08 Kyle of Lochalsh to Inverness service, as Class 27/1 No. 27108 approaches Rose Street junction on 6th June 1981. Class 27s lost their last passenger diagrams in 1986 but the remnants lingered on working a variety of freight and Departmental duties until August 1987.

Situated 191 yards from Rose Street box, this lattice post bracket signal used to protect the approach to Inverness station on the Up Main from Clachnaharry (see Plate 70). It was a coincidence that No. 7 signal (extreme left) read to platform 7, while No. 6 (at proceed) governed movements into platform 6. To its right, No. 5 signal applied to platform 5 and the tallest arm, No. 3 read along the Up Main to Welsh's Bridge cabin. Semaphore signals finally disappeared from Inverness on 21st March 1987 when Rose Street, possibly the most difficult box in the area to operate, was closed, and its layout, suitably modified, controlled from the new PSB (see Plate 209).

Plate 7
The locomotive-hauled two-hourly frequency stopping service connecting Glasgow with Dundee was discontinued on 16th May 1982. Two weeks before it ceased, Class 26 No. 26034 accelerates out of Stirling with the 15.39 Dundee to Glasgow Queen Street service on 1st May 1982.

In its prime, this magnificent gantry, 138 yards south of Stirling Middle box, carried a total of eleven semaphores. Its left-hand extension used to support three signals applying to the Down Loop Siding and the Down Loop, both of which passed beneath the projection and have since been lifted. To the right of the tallest arm, No. 82 Down Main Home signal, was No. 48 reading to the Down S. & D. line (platform 6), while No. 25 (arm removed) applied to platform 10 line. Stirling South's Up Main Distant used to be below No. 71 Up Main Starter (at clear), below which was No. 74 shunt-ahead signal (see Plate 24). No. 66 (miniature arm signal) governed movements from the Up Main to the Up Loop, while on the extreme right, No. 31 was the Up Loop Starter. The gantry was abolished on 9/10th February 1985.

Plate 8
On 27th April 1984, Class 45/1 No. 45139 restarts 4O95, the 14.54 Aintree to Southampton Maritime Container Terminal service, past Bootle Junction. (At Edge Hill, the 'Peak' was relieved by a 25kV ac electric locomotive.) Since the closure of the Aintree Container Terminal on 28th February 1986, the Metal Box siding at Aintree remains the only revenue-earning terminal on the 4 mile 16 chain branch. The Dock branch (on the right), which was singled when the area was resignalled (see below), leads to the remaining north Liverpool Freightliner Terminal at Seaforth.

At Bootle Junction, there were two double junctions, facing from the Southport direction, one connecting the Goods lines (left) to the Main lines (to the right of the locomotive), and the other linking the Main to the Dock lines (on the far right). No doubt observing the 15 mph PSR through No. 9 points, the driver was travelling from the Down Goods, crossing momentarily via the electrified Main lines towards Atlantic Dock Junction. A new structure replaced Bootle Junction box on 13th April 1986, when track remodelling and resignalling rendered the gantry redundant. From left to right, the signals were the Down Goods fixed stop (see Plate 40), and below No. 3 Down Goods Calling-on towards Bank Hall; No. 5 Down Goods to Down Main; No. 6 (in the off position); No. 11 Down Main Home; and No. 12 Down Main to Atlantic Dock Junction.

Plate 9
The Redland Roadstone quarry at Mountsorrel supplies several private companies with aggregates as well as BR with ballast. In this instance, a southbound Departmental departure passes Bell Lane as it approaches Leicester. The train, composed of eight loaded "Sealions", is being hauled by Class 31/1 No. 31296 on 30th July 1984.

The Leicester Gap – an oasis of mechanical signalling in a desert of MAS bounded by West Hampstead and Trent PSBs – was finally filled on 7th December 1987. With the opening of Leicester PSB on 29th June 1986 however came the closure of Bell Lane cabin, hiding behind the right-hand stanchion of this cantilevered gantry some 900 yards north of Leicester station. It used to control movements on the Down passenger line (No. 23 signal at proceed), and from the Down Goods via a series of crossovers to the No. 1 Down Reception line (No. 9 miniature arm signal) [see Plate 21], to the Down Passenger line (No. 8 signal), and along the Down Goods (No. 6). On the right was No. 12 Up Goods Starting with Leicester North distant below, and No. 7 miniature arm reading to the Up Reception line. The train was travelling along the Up Passenger line under the authority of No. 28 Home signal and Leicester North distant at clear, on the bracket north of the box.

Plate 10
On 24th April 1984, two Class 503 emu 3-car sets, (Nos 28680, 29710 and 29279 + 29132, 29841 and 28372), approach Rock Ferry with the 09.26 terminating service from Liverpool Moorfields. (It was not until 30th September 1985 that the electrified passenger service was extended to Hooton.) The Mersey lines run parallel to the former quadruple ex-LNW/GW main line until the electrified lines go underground just to the south of Green Lane junction. The Slow lines eventually joined up with the Mersey Docks & Harbour Board system and the Fast lines terminated at Birkenhead Woodside. In the early 1960s through passenger services to Paddington, Euston, Bournemouth and Barmouth/Pwllheli still passed under this gantry.

At Rock Ferry, track remodelling, allowing through running between James Street and Hooton, and resignalling was commissioned on 19th May 1985, resulting in the demise of this LNW design gantry, a style perpetuated by the LMS, at the northern approaches to the station. Here the Up and Down Goods lines from Green Lane Junction (in the right background) converged to form a bi-directional single line avoiding the station to the east and used to connect via No. 21 crossover points with the Up and Down Mersey lines from Birkenhead Central. The train was passing No. 17 Down Mersey Home signal at clear, about to enter platform 4 via No. 12 facing crossover. On the centre doll was No. 19 signal leading to platform No. 3, while on the right, No. 57 Up Goods Home read to the single line by-passing the station. Below each main arm was a calling-on signal.

Plate 11
A Class 101 dmu (car Nos 53162 and 51246), passes Bog Hall with the 14.20 Whitby to Darlington service on 16th June 1984. This was the site of the junction with the short section to Prospect Hill along which locomotive hauled trains for Scarborough were propelled up the steeply graded line to avoid running-round at West Cliff station. In 1964 Mr Ernest Marples, the Minister of Transport, reprieved the Esk Valley route but endorsed the closure of the Scarborough and Malton lines. The route to Middlesbrough, via Staithes, had succumbed in 1958.

The NE was the largest pre-Grouping railway company to purchase signalling equipment from contractors, and McK&H of Worcester eventually became their largest supplier. Here at Bog Hall Junction, is a typical McK&H product, a lattice steel overhanging bracket, probably erected in 1910 and dismantled in 1985. It was required because there was insufficient space to accommodate a structure on the River Esk side of the line where there were originally extensive sidings. The right-hand arm was No. 4

Up Main Second Home signal towards Sleights, while the left-hand doll used to carry No. 3 signal and read via No. 19 facing crossover on to the single line climbing to Prospect Hill box and thence to Whitby (West Cliff) and Middlesbrough. Bog Hall cabin was switched out at the time this photograph was taken. It was closed on 30th September 1984 and has since been demolished along with the bracket signal.

Plate 12
The 8M64 service from Healey Mills to Carlisle, hauled by Class 25/2 No. 25181 comes off the ex-L&Y route from Wakefield Kirkgate at Goose Hill Junction on 27th May 1981. This service was discontinued when freight traffic over the Settle & Carlisle line ceased in 1983, and traffic was transferred to ECML Speedlink services. The train is taking the Down Slow line to Altofts Junction which was taken out of use on 31st January 1988. Likewise the ex-MR main line to Oakenshaw South Junction (left) – which had been reduced from four tracks to two on 1st May 1967 – was closed completely on 1st June 1987.

Goosehill Junction, about half a mile south of Normanton, boasted two gantries until their demolition in connection with the removal of the junction and the partial abandonment of the former Midland Railway quadruple track route south to Cudworth (see Plate 56), resulting in the closure of Goosehill box on 2nd October 1988. The northern one, illustrated here, spanned the Up (left) and Down Main lines, just south of the box, at one time supported four dolls with nine signal arms. The original left- hand doll, since removed, carried three arms directing movements onto the Up Goods. St. John's Colliery cabin's Up Main Outer Distant used to be mounted below No. 60 Up Main Home; to its right was No. 57, applying Up Main to Up Branch with Lockes Siding cabin's distant below. On the extreme right was No. 52 Up Goods Inner Home, with Lockes Siding No. 36 distant beneath (see Plate 20). Approaching from Wakefield Kirkgate, the train has passed No. 2 Down Branch Home signal, mounted on the other gantry.

Plate 13
A decade has passed since this assemblage was seen at Scarborough on 16th August 1980. Taking pride of place, at platform 1, Class 40 No. 40030 stands at the head of the 13.00(SO) to Manchester Victoria train while Class 31/1 No. 31302 waits to leave platform 2 with the 12.30(SO) to Leicester (via Bridlington) working. The Class 101 dmu is departing with the 12.08 service for York as Class 03 No. 03089 propels empty stock back into the terminus.

One of the signal engineers of the NE, Arthur Hurst, was well-known for his penchant for providing a signal for every conceivable movement at a complicated junction, yard or station. As a result, at its zenith around 1910, the NE boasted a magnificent collection of gantries, brackets, and other structures individually designed for each location. The configuration of signals on the Scarborough station throat gantry, erected in 1903, was altered in 1951, to incorporate, below No. 36 Calling-on signal, a 7-way route indicator, reading from 'C' Road (on which the unit is departing) to all nine platforms, except Nos 1 and 2. Previously there had been seven separate miniature arm shunt signals for each route, and a total of fourteen signals on the gantry. It was taken out of use on 21st October 1984.

Plate 14
The four tracks between Millbrook and Southampton Central station came into existence when the station was rebuilt with four platforms in 1934. The former Down platform was rebuilt as an island and a new platform was built – from which this photograph was taken – for Down services. The tracks under the gantry date from the same period while to the left of the train is the Up Through line which, prior to the rebuilding, was the Down line. The train, the 06.00(FX) Weymouth Quay to Waterloo service hauled by a Class 73 electro-diesel is approaching Southampton Central in August 1980. Having latterly only run during the summer, the boat train was discontinued at the end of the 1985 timetable. Patronage had fallen to such a level, that during 1986 and 1987 the service for the Quay was just an extension of an existing Waterloo to Weymouth Town working. In 1988 it was axed in favour of a bus connection.

This splendid, much photographed gantry at the west end of Southampton Central station carried the Down Starting signals for the Bay Platform (left), the Local (centre) and the Through lines. The signal posts were arranged in groups of three, corresponding to the three different routes available from each line. The lowest three arms were all of SR origin, corrugated to give greater strength and rigidity to the arm. The gantry was taken out of service on 7th November 1981, when Southampton box was closed, but it was carefully dismantled and transported to York for eventual display at the National Railway Museum.

Plate 15
Class 207 demu No. 1305 (since renumbered No. 207005) approaches Tunbridge Wells West with the 09.37 Eridge to Tonbridge service on 23rd August 1983. Consent to close the section between Birchden Junction and Grove Junction was given on 7th February 1985. The final passenger services ran on 6th July 1985 but the route continued to be used for several weeks afterwards to allow access to the carriage sidings (left). It is interesting to recall that in 1969 the Minister of Transport reprieved this line and the section between Oxted and Uckfield.

At the west end of Tunbridge Wells West station stood this modest gantry with the starting signals from the Up Loop (left), the Up Main, the Down Main and the Down Bay (right) latterly to Birchden Junction. The two signals on the Down side read through a trailing crossover (fitted with a facing point lock [see Plate 62] for the use of passenger trains) to the Up Main. Tunbridge Wells West "A" box (formerly named No. 1) was an early SR replacement of an adjacent ex-LBSC cabin, the track layout being generally retained like for like. The box contained a 45 lever, EOD, 4in centres frame, secondhand from either Waterloo or London Bridge, and was closed with the line on 12th August 1985.

2 : Principles of Semaphore Signalling

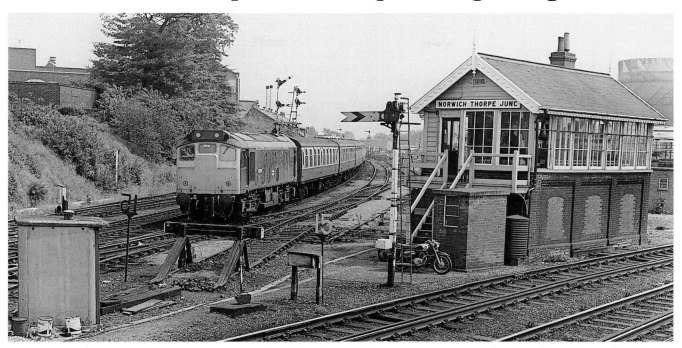

Plate 16

For various reasons the new timetable, due to commence on 11th May 1981, was deferred until 1st June. On 30th May, the penultimate day of the extended period, Class 25/1 No. 25035 drifts past Norwich Thorpe heading the 12.52(SO) Yarmouth to Peterborough service. This locomotive survived until the last official date for withdrawal of the class – 15th March 1987 – although several managed to last for up to eight days more! The closure, and subsequent demolition, of the cabin in July 1986 has left an uninterrupted view of the new Crown Point depot (beginning to take shape on the right).

Instantly recognisable by its yellow arm, with fish-tail end and black chevron, a distant signal indicates caution, i.e. be prepared to stop at the next signal, and may be passed in the position illustrated. When in the clear position (arm raised 45°) all other stop signals worked from the same signal box are clear. At night, the respective indications are yellow light (caution) and green light (proceed). Such factors as the gradient and curvature of the line, and the maximum line speed dictate the positioning of a distant signal, which must always be at full braking distance from the stop signals to which it applies. This is Trowse Swing Bridge cabin's Up Main Distant, which coincidentally happens to be situated adjacent to Norwich Thorpe Junction box. Because of the sharp curvature of the main lines, the signal is equipped with an electric motor, housed in the black and white cabinet near the foot of the post, thus relieving the signalman of a heavy pull.

Plate 17

On 24th July 1984 a Class 108 dmu (car Nos 51945 and 52088) enters Rufford – the only passing loop on the 13 mile Ormskirk line – with the 15.15 service from Preston. Within a couple of months of the diversion of Anglo-Scottish services from Liverpool Exchange to Lime Street stations in May 1970, the former L&Y route south of Midge Hall was singled. The rationalisation was later extended to Farington Curve Junction, leaving the former mainline as a branch. (In September 1985 all through services between Merseyside and Scotland were discontinued.)

Stop signals consist of a red arm with a square end and a vertical white stripe near the outer left-hand end, while the rear is white with a vertical black stripe in a similar position. At night, when the arm is as shown in the horizontal danger (= stop or on) position, the glass spectacle shows a red light; with the arm raised or lowered 45° (hence Upper and Lower Quadrant signals), to indicate proceed (= clear or off), a green light is displayed. Stop signals, classified as home signals, are installed to protect stations, junctions and as shown here both a level crossing and the entrance to a section of line. Rufford's No. 5 Up Main Starting (or section) signal governs the admission of a train onto the single line section to the next stop signal in advance, the Up Home at Midge Hall. A section of line like this is called a block section. Incidentally, on 6th November 1988, No. 5 signal was demolished and replaced by a reflectorised "Stop" board (see Plate 40), positioned 27 yards from the level crossing.

Plate 18
Hurst Green Junction to Uckfield is one of the few non-electrified routes on the Southern Region. The 19 mile section between Hever and Uckfield was singled in January 1990, concentrating all traffic on the former Up line. The Tunbridge Wells and Eridge Railway Preservation Society (TWERPS) is at present negotiating with BR to use the former Down line between Birchden Junction and Eridge. On 19th April, 1984, Eridge was still a delightful rural junction as Class 207 demu No. 1304 (since renumbered 207004) was departing with the 09.31 for London Bridge. This train would combine at Oxted with the 09.46 service from East Grinstead.

This equal balanced bracket signal at the London end of Eridge station controlled the exit from the Up Loop platform (left) and the Up Main platform. The fact that the heights of the signal arms are the same indicates that these signals applied to two different lines and were not junction (or directing) signals — see Plates 31, 32 and 33. Until September 1930, there were cabins at each end of Eridge station — this, the former North box, a S&F Type 5 design, of 1880 closed in January 1990, when resignalling of the Uckfield branch, controlled from the 1987 Oxted SSI panel box, was commissioned.

Plate 19
The extension of the Light Rail Transit system from Manchester to Bury will result in the demise of the ageing Class 504 2-car emus, an example of which, (car Nos 77176 and 65455), approaches Crumpsall on Easter Bank Holiday Monday, 1987, forming the 13.15 Bury to Manchester Victoria service. The vision of a rail-link between north and south Manchester is not new. As early as 1865, it was planned to connect London Road (renamed Piccadilly on 12th September 1960) with Victoria. A century later, the idea was resurrected, when in 1967 a working party reported on the feasibility of the so-called "Picc-Vic" scheme.

The BR Rule Book (Section K – formerly the famous Rule 55) states that when a train is detained at a stop signal showing Danger, the signalman must be reminded of its position. In clear weather, this can be ach-ieved in a number of different ways; for example, by the driver sounding the horn; or by one of the train-crew (either the secondman or the guard, whoever is the nearer) walking to the box; or by the operation of a track circuit – an electrical means for displaying the train's presence to the signalman. In places where the line is track-circuited, the stop signal carries a white diamond-shaped plate, indicating to the train-crew that the signal (in this case Crumpsall's No. 19 Down Main Home) is exempt from Rule K3, and that, except for excessive delay, they need take no further action in advising the signalman of their presence, (see Plate 195). Modified instructions apply during fog or falling snow.

Plate 20
Class 413 (4-CAP) emu No. 3213 enters Goring-by-Sea as it ambles along the south coast with the 09.00 Littlehampton to Brighton local service on 27th August 1983. The 4-CAPs came into existence the previous year by the amalgamation of two 2-HAPs. The one shown is the last of the 1951 build.

When two cabins are close together and thus the block section is only a short distance, the distant signal of the box in advance is often placed below the starting signal of the box in rear. To prevent the distant arm from showing Clear when the stop arm above

is at Danger, a mechanical device – called a slot – is provided on the signal post. In the Goring – Angmering block section however, there was an intermediate gate box at Ferring Crossing, which because of its proximity to Goring, was provided with two Down Distant signals, known as the Outer and Inner Distants. Mounted below Goring's No. 5 Down Main Starter is Ferring's Down Outer Distant, fitted with a Westinghouse E2 10v electric motor, because of its considerable distance from the gate box. The commissioning of the Lancing re-signalling scheme has seen the replacement of the gates by barriers, the semaphores by colour lights, and the abolition of the cabin.

Plate 21
Class 47/3 No. 47319 cautiously approaches Weston Rhyn with the 7F08 Dee Marsh to Warrington Speedlink service on 23rd July 1984. The locomotive had moved light from Wrexham Watery Road to Chirk to pick up the two Cargowaggons. The Up Goods Loop at Weston Rhyn was the first location that the locomotive could run round. Since 28th November 1988, a regular service, 6F48, has run direct from Chirk Kronospan Private Siding to Walton Old Junction but was diverted to Bescot from July 1990.

Elevated shunting signals are provided to direct a (non-passenger carrying) train from a running line to a siding, or vice-versa, or between one running line and another. Controlling shunting operations and lower-speed movements, they come in a deliberate variety of shapes and colour schemes and are thus readily distinguishable from running signals. At the entrance to a goods loop, for example, an arm of reduced dimensions, having the same livery and indications as a running signal, is employed. Here, at Weston Rhyn, is the rear of No. 44 Up Main to Up Goods Loop (lower quadrant) signal, authorising admittance to the loop line. Admire the lovely pole route and note the Fogman's hut – two features fast disappearing from the railway scene.

Plate 22
On 22nd July 1985, a Class 101 dmu passes Brampton Fell as wet weather approaches from the east. The first Metropolitan-Cammell Carriage & Wagon Co. Ltd 2-car units entered public service on 6th February 1956 and boasted seating for 12 1st and 105 3rd class(!) passengers. (It was not until June 1956 that the designation was changed to 2nd class.) Today, with the exception of those units which operate along the Thames Valley and on the Tonbridge-Redhill-Gatwick/Reading route, the majority are exclusively economy class. Another indicator of social change is the proportion of non-smoking accommodation. When delivered, this was limited to twelve, i.e. identical to that allocated to 1st class passengers!

At the exit from a siding or more often a goods loop, another miniature arm semaphore signal, with small red and green spectacles, is usually provided. This outlet signal (from the Up Refuge Siding – formerly the Up Goods Loop – at Brampton Fell), when cleared, permits movements towards the Up Main Starter for the block section to Low Row box, nearly four miles away. These lattice steel McK&H signals were originally lower quadrants, and have had their finials removed. Note the position of the Refuge Siding trap points – to divert errant runaway vehicles from fouling the main line, see *LNERS* Plate 143, for an interior view of Brampton Fell box.

Plate 23
An immaculate Stratford-based Class 37/0 No. 37049 stables in Whitby's platform 1 at the head of "The Whitby Venturer" on 16th June 1984. This privately sponsored excursion for employees of the Ciba-Geigy company had started from the private sidings at Duxford, but returned to the nearby Whittlesford station. Since this photograph was taken, all the other tracks in the station have been lifted.

Usually in the form of small white semaphore arms with horizontal red stripes, subsidiary signals, where provided, are placed below the main signal arm. Although identical in appearance, there are three varieties: Calling-on (or Draw-ahead), Shunt-ahead, and Warning, each with a different meaning, and exhibiting the letters C, S, or W as the case may be. When cleared, the Calling-on signal allows the driver to pass the main arm at Danger, informs him that the line towards the next stop signal (or buffer stop, when there is no signal in advance), is occupied, and he should proceed cautiously prepared to stop short of any obstruction. At Whitby, lever No. 5 (controlling platform 1 Down Direction Draw-ahead signal) would have been pulled when, say, it was necessary to couple up an incoming dmu to one already placed in platform 1 at the buffer stops.

Plate 24
Prior to the closure of the East Lincolnshire line to Spalding via Boston, Garden Street was where the through services from King's Cross joined the ex-GC route. The construction of a spur (opened on 1st March 1965) between the ECML and the Nottingham–Lincoln line at Newark facilitated the diversion of the trains via Lincoln and Barnetby. Passing the site of the former junction, Class 101 dmu (cars 54349 and 51215), approaches Grimsby Town with the 13.55 Cleethorpes to Sheffield (via Gainsborough Central) working on 2nd September 1987.

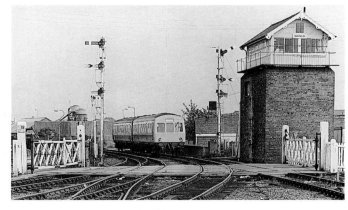

The rear of a Calling-on signal, and its associated route indicator, can be seen next to Garden Street cabin. When photographed, the signal was worked by two separate levers, reading Down Main to Down Back Platform (lever 34), and to Down Main (lever 36) – each with a distinguishing letter indication (B or M respectively), appearing in the route indicator. On the left, the Up Main subsidiary signal used to read three ways, serving as a Calling-on, Warning, and Shunt-ahead signal, but only the latter function is now in use. Subsidiary signals are provided for shunting movements on running lines in the same direction as the normal flow of traffic. Garden Street signal box is a MS&L Type 2 design of 1880 (see Plate 103).

Plate 25

In its final year on the Central Division, Class 413 (4-CAP) emu No. 3209 pulls out of Hove with the 10.32 Portsmouth Harbour to Brighton local service on 26th August 1983. All 4-CAPs were transferred to Ramsgate for work on the South Eastern Division in 1984.

Another type of shunting signal is the ground disc signal – a white metal circle with a horizontal red stripe in appearance. When turned through 45° (resembling the action of a semaphore arm) to the "off" position, the disc face shows a red or green light at night. Its purpose is to control slow-speed shunting movements which are opposite (or trailing) to the general direction of traffic. Outside Hove (formerly Hove "A") box, closed on 16th March 1985, stood No. 14 signal, a Westinghouse pattern ground disc (see *SS*, Fig.20), protecting No. 23 trailing crossover. The rear of an elevated disc (to improve the sighting for the driver) is visible above the leading cab of the emu.

Plate 26

Two Class 202 6-car demus restart the 09.45 Charing Cross to Hastings train out of Wadhurst on 19th April 1984. (The trailing unit, No. 1018, survived to participate in the "Hastings DEMU Farewell" railtour on 11th May 1986.) Three months after the photograph was taken, work on electrification began. Wadhurst Tunnel was singled in September 1985, and the full electrified services commenced in May 1986.

The white diamond painted on the red stripe of this Westinghouse style ground disc (see also *SS*, Plate 82), has the same meaning as the enamel diamond sign attached to the stop signal in Plate 19. This signal, No. 11, read two ways: Shunting Up Main to Up Siding or along the Up Main to the next disc signal No. 8 protecting trailing crossover No. 7 in the distance. Ground discs are commonly found at the entrance to and exit from connections trailing into the main running line, where their provision is much cheaper than miniature arm semaphore signals, and where their size allows their positioning in the six-foot, clear of the structure gauge, as shown here. A BR(ER) example with a diamond sign is illustrated in Plate 33.

Plate 27
The first Metropolitan-Cammell dmu to appear in Scotland arrived early in 1956. It was loaned by the Eastern Region and allocated to Leith Central for crew training. The example depicted, unit No. 101302 (cars 50197, 59303 and 50120) approaches Stirling on 1st May 1982 with the 17.07 Dunblane to Edinburgh train. At the time, the Devon Valley route (right) was in-situ as far as Charlestown Junction (Dumfermline), but the section between Alloa and Longannet Power Station was mothballed. The latter has since been closed and the now-singled stub is solely used to supply the Distillers Company Ltd at Menstrie and Cambus.

Ground disc signals, coloured black with horizontal yellow stripe, are another kind of stop signal. Generally sited at the exit from a siding to a running line, where an overlap shunt spur is provided, they exhibit a yellow or green light during the hours of darkness, and when cleared, the face rotates through 45°, authorising a movement through the crossovers from the Down Sidings to the Down Main. This type of signal however may be passed any number of times in the "on" position, as shown, when shunting movements towards the buffer stops and back, not affecting the main line, are required. The Down Main Home signal (with co-acting arms – see Plate 49) was renewed as a conventional single arm signal in April 1988.

Plate 28
A Metro-Cammell 2-car dmu (cars 50231 and 56404 since renumbered 53231 and 54404) approaches Wearmouth Junction on 2nd March 1982 with the 12.35 Newcastle to Sunderland local service. As a result of funding by the Passenger Transport Executive the service between the two towns has doubled since 1975.

Occasionally, a miniature arm semaphore signal, painted yellow with a vertical black stripe, is employed as an alternative method to convey the same meaning to the driver as the yellow disc signal in Plate 27. Wearmouth's No. 25 Down Sidings to Down Main signal could be passed in this position for shunting moves towards the buffer stops, but for access to the Down Main via No. 26 points, the signal had to be cleared. The stop arm on the right-hand bracket was No. 33 Down Main Starter (released by Line Clear from East Boldon) [see Plate 129]. No. 25 signal was abolished in March 1983 and the remaining signals were removed in October 1984 when Wearmouth box was closed and TCB regulations were introduced between East Boldon and Monkwearmouth cabins.

Plate 29
The trackwork at Kirkham is still impressive despite the closure of the "New Line" to Blackpool Central in November 1965. (This opened in 1903 to give a more direct route into Blackpool and provide more platform space for the masses of holidaymakers escaping from the mill towns of Lancashire and Yorkshire.) Several clues show where the former Up line from Blackpool Central joined the Up Fast at Kirkham North Junction. Notice the acute angle of the signal box to the main line and the graded earthwork leading to the abutment that lifted the Up Central line over the route to Blackpool North and Fleetwood via Poulton. This view on 6th August 1987, shows a Derby Suburban Class 116 dmu, allied to a Class 101 set approaching the station with the 13.00 Blackpool North to Manchester Victoria train.

In some places, a shunting ground disc reads to two or more different lines, and a small indicator (generally of the stencil type) is provided to inform the driver of his route. When the signal is cleared, one of the stencil indications (either a letter or a figure, or sometimes a combination of both) is lit, which is selected mechanically (by the position of the determining points) and electrically. At Kirkham (formerly North), No. 33 disc (lower right foreground) reads three ways via No. 56 trailing crossover from the bi-directionally signalled Up & Down Slow, on which the dmu is approaching: to the Up & Down Lytham single line – to Blackpool South (far left), stencil route indication "L", the Tip (centre left) or the Down Fast (past the tall starting signal in the left background).

Plate 30
The first Class 142 railbuses entered public service on 30th September 1985 working from Newton Heath depot. A week after this, on 7th October, the Department of Transport approved a further £24 million expenditure on 'Pacers'. This involved 46 more Class 142 and 23 Class 144 sets. This view depicts Class 142 No. 142050 – the last of the initial batch – combined with No. 142088 entering Hellifield with the 17.18 Leeds to Morecambe service on 6th August 1987. (No. 142050 was unique in being fitted with Voith hydraulic transmission when new.)

In older installations, disc signals may be placed one above the other. The direction of route is given by the vertical disposition of the signals. Thus the top disc applies to the line on the extreme left, the second to the line next in order from the left and so on. Generally not more than three disc signals are arranged in this manner. Here at Hellifield South, the top disc (No. 27) reads from the Down Main platform (left) across to the Up Main towards Skipton while No. 53 (bottom) applies to the Up Branch towards Blackburn (right) via Nos 47, 48 and 49 points.

Plate 31
The trackbed in the foreground is the former Down Slow at the east end of Abergele & Pensarn station. It was not a casualty of the recent £300 million A55 road widening but was lifted at the end of the 1960s when nearly all the four-track sections west of Chester were eliminated. Quadrupling of the section was completed in 1903 as a consequence of the greatly increased tourist traffic on the North Wales coast. (The quadruple section through the station survived until December 1988 when the Up Main was lifted.) The train, hauled by Class 25/3 No. 25268, is a Departmental working on 13th August 1985 bound for Penmaenmawr. Because of its good mechanical condition, this locomotive was designated one of the twelve Class 25/9s the following December, and was renumbered No. 25902. It remained in traffic until March 1987.

Route indication is also given by the arrangement and stepping of semaphore signals, the highest arm always applying to the straight (or highest speed) route, while the lower arms for the diverging routes read either to the right or left. Therefore a separate stop signal is provided for each particular route. At Abergele, the higher arm (No. 2 Down Main Home) reads straight on through the centre of the station while No. 4 Down Main to Down Slow (the platform line) authorises a lower-speed divergence to the left. By night, the relative disposition of the red and green lights indicates the route set up.

Plate 32
A westbound local service leaves Shoreham-by-Sea formed from emu No. 6033 in August 1979. Prior to its withdrawal in 1966, this was where the route to Christ's Hospital diverged from the Coast line. When photographed, although no longer a through route, the southern end of the branch was retained to serve the Blue Circle cement works at Beeding. When traffic ceased the line was mothballed but formal closure was delayed until March 1988.

At most diverging points, the signals are placed on a bracket overhanging to the right or left, depending on the layout of the junction. At Shoreham-by-Sea "B", formerly Shoreham West box, No. 5 Down Main Home signal for the principal route has been cleared, while No. 7 Down Main to Down Branch Home signal (for the former Beeding branch) is bracketed out to the right. Here again, the scene has changed almost beyond all recognition: on 15th September 1985, the gates were replaced by power-worked MCB (see Plate 130). Since the closure of the cabin on 15th May 1988, they are now worked by the signalman at Lancing with the aid of CCTV (see Plate 132). The semaphores have given way to colour lights, and the Beeding branch has finally been abandoned.

Plate 33
Surrounded by the Departmental Up (left) and Down sidings at Barnetby on 31st March 1989, Class 47/0 No. 47277 heads 6S32, the 10.51 Immingham Norsk Hydro to Leith South company train. It is composed of seven (TOPS code) IPA wagons that were delivered in 1986. Each weekday, two other trains leave the Norsk Hydro terminal. Overnight, departs the 6V40 company train while for Hallen Marsh the 6D58 Speedlink for Doncaster Belmont leaves in the afternoon.

Three 3-doll balanced bracket signals are needed at Wrawby Junction for the Down Fast, the Down Slow and Down Goods lines from Barnetby, which diverge three ways to Doncaster, Gainsborough and Lincoln. No. 130 signal, the Down Fast Home to Doncaster, shows a proceed aspect and warns of a right-hand divergence, while its partners No. 123 Down Fast Home to Gainsborough – the tallest arm pointing out the highest speed route – and No. 113 Down Fast Home to Lincoln, indicating a left-hand route, remain at Danger. Similarly, the three-doll bracket in the centre is the Down Slow Home to Doncaster, Gainsborough and Lincoln respectively, and the bracket signal on the right applies to the Down Goods reading the same three ways. With a 137 lever frame, Wrawby Junction box is the second largest mechanical cabin on BR.

Plate 34
Class 56 No. 56025 approaches Shireoaks East Junction with the 7F47 mgr service from Oxcroft Colliery to Cottam Power Station on 27th May 1987. ("F" services are bound for Cottam whereas "G" indicates West Burton.) Fifteen trains were scheduled to service Cottam that day, delivering a total of 16,000 tonnes of coal originating from the mines at Creswell, Thoresby, Warsop, Shirebrook, Welbeck, Blidworth and Oxcroft.

This 2-doll balanced bracket signal indicates a left-hand diverging junction and incorporates motor-worked distant signals below the stop arms. On the left-hand doll, the stop arm is Shireoaks East Junction's No. 5 Down Main to Down East Curve Home, while the lower arm is controlled from the panel in Shireoaks Station box and is the motor-worked distant (No. 533A) for the colour light signal (No. 796) protecting Woodend Junction. On the taller doll, Shireoaks East's No. 2 Down Main Home is placed above Shireoaks Station No. 535A Down Main Distant.

Plate 35
Class 20s Nos 20158 and 20136 make a foray onto the Western Region as they prepare to enter Rainbow Hill Tunnel on the approach to Worcester Tunnel Junction on 29th May 1985. The train, composed exclusively of empty Departmental (TOPS code) ZAV wagons, is the 9V01 Bescot Down Section Sidings to Gloucester New Yard service.

This right-hand bracket on the approach to Worcester from the north combines the principles delineated in Plates 21 and 34. The miniature arm shunting signal is worked from Tunnel Junction box by either of two levers. It is provided with a small route indicator (the rectangular apparatus below its arm) to display by means of a letter or number which of the three routes it controls is set up. With lever 48 reversed, the route for the Up Goods is selected; lever 45 however governs two routes: either to the Up Goods Siding or the Up Goods Running Loop. At proceed is

No. 5 Up Main Home signal to Shrub Hill station, the principal route. On its right is No. 7 Up Main to Up Loop reading towards Foregate Street station. Both distant signals are fixed (see Plate 42).

Plate 36
Much of the coal from South West Scotland is taken to Ayr Docks for export to Ireland. In this instance Class 20s Nos 20198 and 20089 are seen coming from the North Quay, on the Harbour branch, on 3rd August 1983. Since this photograph was taken, the Class 20s have been replaced by various combinations usually involving a Class 37 locomotive, and the (TOPS code) HBA wagons have been superseded by HAA hoppers on mgr services. Other changes include the extension of the "Coal" network resulting from the opening of several open-cast sites and the greatly improved discharge facilities at Ayr Harbour.

In a yard or industrial shunting area, there may be a number of diverging routes from a given pair of points, and so several subsidiary shunting signals, used for movements corresponding with the normal flow of traffic, may be needed, one for each of the various routes. Up to five miniature arms (see Plate 97) may be mounted one above another on the same post and, in descending order, the arms read from left to right-hand routes, corresponding in principle to the ground shunting signals in Plate 30. At Ayr Harbour Junction, two 2-arm shunting signals are required to give route indications from the Up Harbour Line (centre road of the five in the foreground) and the Up Docks Line (on which the train is travelling). Both top arms (Nos 17 and 2 respectively) apply to the West Siding, while the lower arms (Nos 20 and 9) refer to the Up Newton Line.

Plate 37
An interesting 3-car dmu stands at Dunblane with the 15.39 departure for Glasgow Queen Street on 24th August 1981. The hybrid is led by Gloucester-built Class 122 single car dmu (No. 55002) and the trailing cars are Class 101 Nos 59303 and 50197.

A repeating signal consists of a small black semaphore arm in a circular glass-fronted frame, with an opaque white background. The arm is square-ended for a stop signal and notched for a distant signal, (see *SS*, Fig. 23). Known as a banner repeater signal, it is placed roughly 50 to 200 yards on the approach side of the signal to which it relates and is illuminated at night. When the signal to which the repeater refers is at Danger, the arm is horizontal; it is inclined 45° up or down (depending on whether the main signal is an upper or lower quadrant), for proceed. At Dunblane, the station footbridge obscures a driver's view of No. 45 Down Main Home signal, (see Plate 223), thus necessitating the provision of this banner repeater (numbered 45R). Years ago, a second repeater used to be fixed to the left of No. 45R, giving advance warning of the signal governing the left-hand divergence onto the former Callander branch.

Plate 38
Engineering work near Darlington required the diversion of services via Stockton on 17th May 1981. Trains left the ECML at Tursdale Junction and followed the Up Slow line to Ferryhill South Junction before taking the freight route via Stillington. One of the affected services, the 11.25 Edinburgh to Plymouth, is seen passing Bishop Middleham hauled by Class 47/4 No. 47429. Prior to 3rd November 1981, when this service became operated by a HST, this train was regularly hauled by a 'Deltic' locomotive north of York. The branch to the Fishburn Coking Plant (since closed) can be seen to the right of the locomotive.

A colour-light distant is often mounted beneath the last semaphore signal preceding the approach to a MAS area, (see also Plate 56). With the semaphore arm at Danger, the colour-light is unlit, but it shows the appropriate aspects with the arm above cleared. Bishop Middleham's No. 19 Up Main Home semaphore arm has been fitted with a red intensified light and the green spectacle removed, (to prevent two green aspects from being given when the arm is "off"), and the colour-light, capable of displaying yellow, double yellow (as in this case) or green aspects, is Ferryhill's (see Plate 203) Up Stockton Distant for F452 signal, the three-aspect colour-light Outer Home, 1,240 yards away. Bishop Middleham box was switched out of circuit, i.e. it was unmanned and its signals cleared, when this photograph was taken, and it was closed on Monday, 30th April 1984.

Plate 39

Electrification west of Brighton came about in three main phases. West Worthing became the temporary terminus in 1933 when the Victoria/Three Bridges/Brighton scheme was extended along the coast. On 26th August 1983, Class 413 (4-CAP) emu No. 3311 leaves West Worthing with the 12.32 Portsmouth Harbour to Brighton service. Through electrified services between these towns resulted from the "third rail" being extended to Havant (part of the Mid-Sussex scheme in 1938), thus linking up with the "Portsmouth Direct line" scheme of 1937.

A "Limit of Shunt" indicator (see *SS,* Fig.12) consists of a square metal board fixed to a post, with the words "Limit of Shunt" (or "Shunt Limit") in red letters on a white background. The indicator is illuminated at night and is actually a permanent stop signal, prohibiting any movement past it. In this example at West Worthing, emus from the Middle Siding at the Goring end of the station (behind the photographer) were authorised by ground disc No. 13 to set back into the Down platform. The "Limit of Shunt" indicator was provided to stop a set-back movement (against the normal flow of traffic) from proceeding over the level crossing and running away wrong-line into the rear block section towards Worthing. No. 5 Up Advance Starter (seen in the "off" position) admits the train to the West Worthing–Worthing block section. West Worthing box closed on 5th June 1988, the crossing being supervised by CCTV from Lancing (see Plate 132).

Plate 40

In February 1981, Class 37/0 No. 37045 restarts a Horden Colliery to Dawdon Colliery working after pausing at Bone Mill level crossing on the Seabanks branch. This unfitted trip, composed of (TOPS code) HTO and HTV 21 tonne hoppers, involved a run-round at Dawdon signal box. Horden Colliery has since been closed and access to the bunker at Dawdon Colliery is directly from the coast route 0 miles 77 chains south of Dawdon box.

The maximum permissible speed on the Seabanks branch is 15 mph and over Bone Mill open level crossing, just to the right of the photographer, (see Plate 139), it is 10 mph. At places where low speeds were required for safety reasons, for example when approaching buffer stops, or in this case, to ensure a driver had his train properly under control when descending the 1 in 267 gradient approaching Dawdon Colliery sidings, a "fixed" stop signal, consisting of a full-size semaphore arm, similar in design to a "fixed" distant (see Plate 42), was provided. When the train had stopped, permission to proceed was granted by the signalman clearing one of the miniature arm signals. No. 18 Up Main First Home (mounted below the "fixed" stop arm) applied along the Up Main towards Seabanks box, some 670 yards away, and No. 33 Up Main First Home to Colliery Line directed trains via Nos 30 and 31 facing points across the Down Main into Dawdon Colliery. The signals were brought into use in August 1978 and were abolished on 25th July 1987 when the Seabanks branch was singled, and Seabanks box closed. They were replaced by a Notice Board worded "Stop. Telephone. If no staff on duty, proceed with caution."

Plate 41
On 1st August 1988, a 3-car Class 144 set No. 144016 – recently reinforced by the addition of an intermediate trailer car – forms the 13.31 Keighley to Leeds service between Apperley Junction and the site of the former Calverley & Rodley station. The ex-MR main line south of Guiseley Junction was quadrupled in sections around the turn of the century. Subsequently the Fast lines – off the photograph to the left – were lifted in 1967, leaving all traffic concentrated on the former Slow lines. Passenger traffic was greatly reduced along the Aire Valley when the local services between Leeds and Bradford were withdrawn in 1965 and all services concentrated on the more direct ex-GN route via Pudsey in 1967.

Today, only one distant signal, applying to all trains approaching it, is provided at a diverging junction. However, it used to be the practice many years ago to install a separate distant signal for each particular route. Such signals, known as "splitting" distants, are only very occasionally found but an example still survives at Apperley Junction, approaching from the Leeds direction. No. 25 (taller arm) is the Down Main Distant for the principal route to Shipley, and No. 27 Down Main to Down Branch Distant gives advance warning of the lower speed right-hand divergence to Ilkley. Note the MR finial crowning one of the dolls.

Plate 42
Propelling a brakevan, Class 08 No. 08113 approaches Bodmin General on 4th August 1982. Before proceeding to Wenford Bridge the locomotive picked up 18 empty (TOPS code) UCV "Clay hood" wagons at Bodmin, and a further 38 at Boscarne Junction. The final revenue earning train left Wenford Bridge in September 1983 and the official closure of the whole branch from Bodmin Road (since renamed Bodmin Parkway) took place in February 1984. The closure of the section beyond Boscarne Junction left Cornwall bereft of any ex-LSW line, although the ex-GW line between Bodmin General and Bodmin Parkway has recently been re-opened as a steam railway.

On some single lines, especially where the traffic is infrequent, or on main lines where a PSR exists, what is known as a "fixed" distant signal is provided at say the approach to a passing loop or junction, respectively. This is an unworked distant arm, permanently exhibiting a caution message. It is not connected by wire to the signal box lever frame, and thus helps to save on maintenance costs.

Plate 43

The present route to Fishguard was opened on 30th August 1906 when the steamer service to Rosslare was inaugurated. This required the construction of a 10 mile 47 chain link between Clarbeston Junction and Letterston Junction. In the foreground is part of the original route via Letterston which was unsuitable as a main line as it was single throughout and for two miles had a 1 in 27 gradient. Presently, 21 chains of this route are used for access to the Trecwn branch. Having negotiated the remains of this route and run-round its train, Class 37/0 No. 37073 leaves Letterston Junction and heads for Whitland with 7B57, the 11.35 Trecwn to Carmarthen Speedlink service on 9th August 1988. The train is composed of (TOPS code) ODA, VBA, VEA and VAA wagons. In the early 1980s Trecwn was serviced by a trip from Llandeilo Junction. The closure of this yard in 1982 resulted in the traffic working to Margam and later to Severn Tunnel Junction. Today all remaining Speedlink traffic for West Wales works from Gloucester New Yard.

Nowadays, the traditional fixed distant is being rapidly supplanted by what is known as the reflectorised distant board. This consists of a rectangular metal board, mounted on a post, with an emblem of a distant signal arm on a white background of retro-reflective material. Having the same meaning as the caution aspect of a semaphore distant signal, this example on the Trecwn branch approaching Letterston Junction, serves to remind the driver that he is about to enter the passing loop, at the end of which is a Stop Board and a pair of trap points. It was brought into use on 13th July 1987, when Letterston Junction box, one of the BR(WR) 'plywood wonders' (see Plate 196), was closed.

Plate 44

Visitors to Barmouth find their way barred by ex-GW 4-6-0 'Manor' class locomotive No. 7819 *Hinton Manor* as it heads the Down "Cardigan Bay Express" into the station on 2nd August 1987. Steam services on the Cambrian Coast ran on several days each week during the summer. All trains originated at Machynlleth; destinations including Aberystwyth, Barmouth and Porthmadog.

Wherever possible, signals are positioned on the left-hand side of the line to which they apply, with the coloured indications (for use at night) as close as possible to the driver's eye level. To the left is Barmouth South's No. 4 Up Main Second Home signal – a typical BR(LMR) restricted height signal – provided because the station awning restricted the driver's view. Barmouth is a passing place and when the photograph was taken the Up line was bi-directionally signalled, i.e. movements

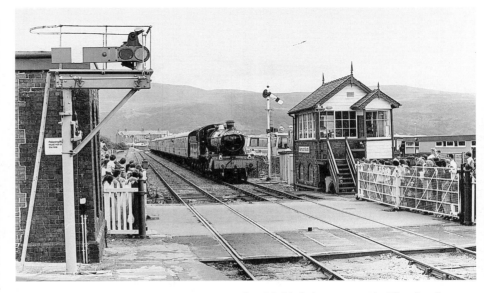

on the Up line could be signalled in both Up or Down directions, see the right-hand bracket signal behind the rear coach. The signals were a mixture of lower and upper quadrants – Barmouth being on the former Cambrian Railways and now BR(LMR). Dating from 1890, the cabin was one of the last operational Dutton Type 1 designs, (see Plates 26 and 77). The level crossing gates were replaced by MCB in February 1988.

Plate 45
Erroneously boasting "Blackpool" as its destination, the 05.27 Carlisle to Lancaster service approaches Millom on 1st August 1985. It is made up of three Class 108 2-car dmus (car Nos 54263, 54249 + 53956, 53973 + 53966, 54238). They have been specially fitted with bars over the windows because of the limited loading gauge on the former Maryport & Carlisle section.

To improve the driver's sighting of this LMS restricted height signal – Millom's No. 4 Down Main Home – part of the stone overbridge has been painted white. On the right, No. 7 signal, a 2-arm ground disc, with diamond signs, reads Shunting Up Main to Down Main (through the trailing crossover) (top disc), and Up Main to Up Sidings (bottom). Millom cabin is a Furness Railway Type 4 design of 1917, with a RSCo (Fazakerley Works), 31 lever, 5½in centres, frame. It works AB to Foxfield (4 miles 1,404 yards) and Silecroft (3 miles 95 yards) distant.

Plate 46
Speeding through the Fenland on 16th April 1984, Class 31/4 No. 31421 passes Brandon with the 13.15 Birmingham New Street to Norwich working. The schedule was reduced by 40 minutes in May 1988 when Class 156 'Super Sprinters' took over these services. The present route of the West Midlands/East Anglia trains via Leicester came into existence on 6th June 1966 when the line between Peterborough East and Rugby Midland was closed.

Where there is no convenient overbridge or other structure in the vicinity, a wooden or metal sight screen or board is provided to improve visibility. Attached to No. 32 Up Home at Brandon is the BR(ER) design of board, whose width is on average 3 feet. In the 1940s this signal used to be a tall right-hand bracket. Built in 1931, Brandon box is a LNER Southern Area Type 11c design, evolved from the GN Type 4b. Most of these cabins were of brick construction, with a boarded (but in a few cases, as here, brick) section in the centre front by the stove. The 40 lever frame is at the rear. All Type 11 boxes had plain bargeboards, short finials, and concrete lintels to the locking room windows. Note the gabled extension to provide the signalman with a clearer view of the road approaches to the level crossing, which is nowadays protected by MCB.

Plate 47
In 1982, several Metro-Cammell 3-car dmus lost their intermediate trailer cars. Detail differences resulted in the newly created Class 111s becoming cheaper to run and maintain. One such set, comprising cars 78972 and 78722, (previously 51545 and 51565), approaches Barnsley on 4th August 1987 with the 13.43 Leeds to Sheffield service. Note the enamel sign, finished in Eastern Region blue.

A different solution to the same problem – this time at the north end of Barnsley station. Again, to improve the sighting because of the intervening station canopy, No. 5 Down Main Home (right) and No. 8 Down Main to Down Dodworth are equipped with shortened arms, thus bringing the lamps as close as possible to the driver's eye level, without fouling the structure gauge. Note the enamelled metal diamond sign is in fact hexagonal in shape and measures some 2 feet 3 inches wide by 12 inches high. Known as Barnsley Exchange Junction until 25th September 1972, Barnsley Station Junction is a L&Y box of 1901, housing a 56 lever frame, manufactured at Horwich Works.

Plate 48
Class 31/1 No. 31109 hauls 6A85, the 14.50 Norwich Yard to Whitemoor Up Yard Speedlink service past Spooner Row on 17th April 1984. Much of the traffic had worked into Norwich via the 9R12 trip from North Elmham. The Polybulks had come from North Elmham and the cement (TOPS code) PCA wagons from Wymondham. Sadly, the cement terminal is no more, and the Dereham branch was closed in June 1989.

Due to the curvature of the line, No. 4 Down Home at Spooner Row is sited on a left-hand bracket on the "wrong" side of the line. It used to be the practice to place Home signals as near as possible to the signal box or level crossing, but today, the Department of Transport requirement at modernised level crossings is that signals protecting the level crossing should be not less than 50 metres from it, (see Plate 127). Spooner Row cabin is a GE Type 2 design, of 1881, with a 15 lever, McK&H frame and gate wheel.

Plate 49
Class 47/0 No. 47064 trundles through Wem with the 6V32 Stanlow to Severn Tunnel Junction oil train on 21st August 1985. All tanks are destined for Exeter Riverside and would be attached to the 6B19 Speedlink service at Severn Tunnel Yard.

In certain locations, what are termed co-acting arms are provided at the extremities of the same signal post, one arm high up with a sky background giving the train crew a long-range view of the signal, the other roughly at driver's eye level (generally 12 feet from rail level), but perhaps obscured from sight until within say 100 to 50 metres or less. Here, at Wem, the lower arm of No. 32 Down Main Starter is provided to obviate the need for the driver to lean out of his cab to observe the upper arm, when re-starting from a station stop. Wem is a LNW Type 4 cabin, dating from 1883, with a 35 lever, Railway Executive Committee (also known as LMS pre-1943) type frame, placed in the rear of the box.

Plate 50
The 11.42 Sheffield to Cleethorpes service passes Friargate Crossing on 2nd September 1987 formed from a Metro-Cammell 2-car dmu. Modernisation is slowly changing the scene but at the beginning of 1990 there were still five gated level crossings in the vicinity of Grimsby Town station!

The Grimsby area is still by and large a haven of mechanical signalling. At Friargate Crossing, a co-acting home and distant is necessary, because of the sharp curvature of the line and the low Deansgate overbridge, from which this picture was taken. F10 signal is Friargate's Down Home, beneath which is No. 13 Down Distant for Littlefield Crossing, visible in the distance, only 227 yards away. Again, to improve the sighting because of the sharp bend, Friargate's No. 2 Up Home, with Wellowgate Crossing's Up fixed distant below, is situated on the "wrong" side of the line. Both cabins are MS&L Type 2 examples of 1884, and retain their original lever frames.

3 : Pre-Grouping (LMS and GWR) Signal Boxes

Plate 51

On 24th August 1987, the Class 150/1 'Sprinter' No. 150130 forming the 13.06 Holyhead to Bangor service fails to generate any custom at Ty Croes. This remote village retained its station during the "Beeching Axe". The nearby, more substantial settlement at Valley lost its passenger service in 1966 due to the proximity of the A5 road and the associated bus services. The original proposal was for eighteen intermediate stations between Chester and Holyhead to be closed. Fortunately, six were reprieved and four have since been re-opened.

At 254 miles 32 chains from Euston, Ty Croes, one of the two surviving S&F cabins on the Chester & Holyhead, is a strong contender for the title of BR's oldest working block post, (but see Plate 144). It is of all-brick construction, with two segmental-arched locking room windows, six-pane operating floor windows, and a hipped roof. Built probably by the LNW circa 1871, when the block system was being inaugurated, it received an 18 lever LNW tumbler frame new in 1901 and, until its demotion to a gatebox on 2nd April 1989, worked AB to Gaerwen and Valley.

Plate 52

Heading the 11.50 Bidston Dock to Fiddlers Ferry Power Station mgr service, Class 47/3 No. 47320 comes off the Mersey Docks & Harbour Company line at Canning Street North on 12th August 1985. A short term contract with the CEGB resulted in the use of this route for moving coal imported through the REA Terminal at Bidston Dock. Three trains ran five/six days a week for six months. The unloading facilities at Bidston Dock were originally opened to supply iron-ore to the former John Summers steelworks at Shotton. Chronic overcapacity in the industry resulted in the rationalisations of the early 1980s and the last iron-ore train ran on 2nd April 1980.

Built over a period of 28 years from 1876, the LNW Type 4 cabin was one of the most numerous of all pre-Grouping box designs, with about 100 still operational today. Apart from the gabled roof, it is similar to the 1875 era Type 3 design. It embodied BTF construction, with S&F style locking room windows, and a timber superstructure of lapped boarding, over which plain bargeboards are fixed. The finials are integral with the bargeboards. Of 4 feet elevation (height of operating floor above rail level), Canning Street North measures roughly 21 feet by 9 feet. Dating from 1900, it controls a now rarely found railway level crossing and associated slip points with an original 18 lever LNW tumbler frame. With the closure of Green Lane box on 3rd December 1986, Canning Street North works directly to Rock Ferry.

Plate 53
In 1966 – when Barbara Castle was the Minister of Transport in the Labour Government – the closure of the extremities of the Birkenhead to Helsby route was proposed. In the event, only the 1½ miles between Rock Ferry and Woodside actually succumbed and the section between Stanlow & Thornton and Helsby was reprieved. On the latter section, Class 101 dmu (cars 54342 and 51184) forms the 11.27 Hooton to Helsby service past Helsby–West Cheshire Junction on 24th April 1984. These trains now run from Chester by reversing at Hooton. The small, but busy, signal box controls access to the Shellstar (UKF) siding (behind the train) and the junction with the freight-only single line to Mouldsworth Junction (foreground). The line became much more important after 16th June 1957 when the BR

(LMR) constructed a 0 mile 29 chain curve (thus creating a triangle at Northwich) between Sandbach Junction South Junction and Sandbach Junction West Junction (since renamed Northwich South and Northwich West Junctions respectively). This created a direct access to Crewe and the Potteries.

Opened in 1900, to house a 36 lever, LNW tumbler frame, with bar and stud locking, Helsby West Cheshire Junction is a standard LNW Type 4 all timber cabin, of size G. The letter size relates to the number of standard window units used on the front of the LNW standardised boxes, in this case 2 + 2 + 3 + 2 (see *LNWRS*, pages 125/6). Notice the wood beams at the rear to resist further movement of the box, and the ground disc signal in the foreground with a diamond sign.

Plate 54
Leaving the Down Slow at Speke Junction, Class 58 No. 58014 heads for Garston Junction on 12th August 1985, while forming 7F47, the 10.42 Toton Old Bank to Garston mgr service. Carrying Nottinghamshire coal for export, the train was running for the first time since the miners' two week holiday. The coal terminal came into use in the summer of 1981 to service the electricity supply industry in Northern Ireland.

The use of a telephoto lens belies the large mass of Speke Junction box, a standard LNW Type 5 design, of 1907. The height (18 feet above rail level) helps to accommodate the mechanical interlocking of the 100 lever frame, which is housed at the rear of the cabin, and also used to provide, until the OLE and wire mesh on the windows were

installed, the signalman with an unimpeded view of the layout he controls. A cantilevered bay window in the centre has also been built for the convenience of the signalman in communicating with train crews. The use of panelled brickwork in signal box construction produced a stronger building than the earlier types illustrated – needed because of the ever-increasing weight of the locking frame – and was very common in large and tall cabins (see Plate 237). The signalman's mode of transport to work rests in the wooden shed adjacent to the coal bunker.

Plate 55

If rumours are to be believed, the misnomer on the signal box will be rectified when the station, closed in 1964, is reopened as part of the passenger service connecting Nottingham, Mansfield and Worksop. On 6th April 1988, 7G76, the 15.39 Warsop Main Colliery to West Burton Power Station mgr service, approaches the former Whitwell station, headed by Class 58 No. 58031.

Almost all Midland boxes were built wholly of timber, with standard prefabricated parts, made up in the Signal Shops. Whitwell is a small Type 2b, dating from 1893. The finials are a standard Midland feature, but the nameboard is the 1935 LMS style, based on Midland practice. It has square ends and beaded edges, with 6 inch cast-iron letters, painted white on a 9in (in this case, BR red) board edged with ¾in white painted bead. Notice the 'No Admittance' sign below the windows at the top of the steps. About 10% of the 500 or so Type 2 boxes are still in use. Whitwell is one of a small minority of Midland boxes not to contain a Midland lever frame; that was replaced in 1953 by the BR(ER) with a McK&H, 4in centres frame of 42 levers.

Plate 56

Class 56 No. 56028 passes the site of Cudworth station and prepares to take the branch to Grimethorpe with an empty mgr train on 1st June 1982. This station was one of the casualties when local services between Leeds City and Sheffield Midland via Wath were axed in 1968. The route remained part of the InterCity network connecting the Midlands with Leeds/Bradford but, one year after the photograph was taken, landslips resulted in these services being re-routed via Moorthorpe. The temporary diversion has since become permanent and this section of the former MR main line is no longer a through route.

The exception to the rule! Cudworth Station South Junction, to give it its full name, was the only known Midland box with a stone base. Quite why this unique form of construction was employed has never been established. However, the cabin, a Type 3b built in 1900, contained a 64 lever Midland tappet frame. When photographed, it worked AB to Cudworth Station Junction, Cudworth South Junction and Stairfoot, and TCB to Sheffield PSB. The colour light signal mounted at the foot of No. 51 Up Main Home signal was capable of showing yellow, double yellow or green aspects when the semaphore was in the clear position.

Plate 57
The "Border City" ran from Paddington to Carlisle on 24th March 1984. The recently renamed and reliveried Class 50 locomotive No. 50007 *Sir Edward Elgar* hauled the train as far as Crewe, from where, Class 40s Nos 40028 (formerly *Samaria*) and 40086 took over for the journey via the Settle & Carlisle line. It is seen drifting into Garsdale with escaping steam – and not low cloud – obliterating most of the train.

An example of a Midland Type 4c box is Garsdale, which replaced two earlier cabins, North and South, on 10th July 1910. Situated on the Down platform in the centre of the layout it controls, Garsdale represents one of the last boxes to be equipped with a tumbler frame (6in pitch), necessitating a 12 feet wide cabin. The 40 lever frame is placed at the rear, a practice begun by the Midland around 1908, to give the signalman a clearer view of the traffic. The windows are replacements, the design being introduced by the LMS in 1933. At the time the photograph was taken, Garsdale was switched out of circuit, the block section being Blea Moor to Kirkby Stephen.

Plate 58
A Swindon built Class 120 dmu approaches Spondon with the 11.06 Birmingham New Street to Nottingham service on 3rd August 1984. Originally built for the BR(WR) cross-country routes, these units were dispersed to other regions after the rash of closures in the early 1960s. When new, the centre car had the luxury of a miniature buffet. After a gap of 30 years, similar facilities have been revived on many "Express" Provincial services. In September 1986, the BR(LMR) transferred the last of its passenger allocation from Chester to Ayr depot.

Another rare Midland design was Spondon Station box, built in 1918, to Type 4d. It was a deliberate experiment by the company's Chief Engineer, W.B. Worthington, with new materials and included a BTF base, and concrete corner posts. This form of non-standard construction was not perpetuated by Worthington's successor, James Briggs, who did not favour it. By this time too, the provision of decorative finials, so common to Midland cabins, had ceased through wartime shortages of skilled labour and materials. Latterly reduced to a ground frame, Spondon was closed in December 1988.

Plate 59
Two 3-car Class 501 emus vacate the Broad Street terminus with the 15.14 departure for Richmond on 11th July 1981. After the extension of the North London "third-rail" electrification in May 1985, the Richmond services were diverted to North Woolwich. Broad Street finally closed in June 1986 when the remaining peak period Watford trains were re-routed to Liverpool Street. The last Class 501s in public service were withdrawn in October 1985.

When Broad Street station was re-signalled in 1876, two new cabins were provided situated opposite each other at the country end of the platforms. Upon closure of No. 1 box, which controlled the No. 1 pair of lines on the quadruple track section from the station, the layout was concentrated in No. 2 box, seen here, which used to signal the No. 2 pair of lines. It was a North London Railway Type 1 design, opened on 3rd September 1876, with a 37 lever frame. Around 1890, the cabin was extended at the country end to accommodate a 70 lever, Stevens frame, subsequently enlarged to 73 levers. Today, the scene has changed completely and all traces of Broad Street station and No. 2 box have been obliterated.

Plate 60
When this photograph was taken on 5th August 1987, the freight network around Leek Brook Junction was still busy. The train featured, 8K13, the 14.45 Leek Brook Junction to Longport service, is being hauled by Class 31/1 No. 31234 through Milton Junction. It had earlier worked in two portions from Caldon Low (Tarmac) Quarry and would later continue as the 8K42 service to the Witton stone terminal. (Note the [TOPS code] MCV wagons. This train remained vacuum braked right to the end.) Traffic from Caldon Low ceased on 8th February 1989, and the last train from Oakamoor ran on 30th August 1988. The trackbed diverging to the left originally went to Upper Junction via Biddulph, the last section of which closed in 1979.

Only ten weeks after closure on 20th May 1987, Milton Junction, on the former North Staffordshire Railway, still presented a reasonable appearance, despite much evidence of the permanent way alterations and signalling abandonments associated with the singling of the line (using the former Down line) from Glebe Street Junction (Stoke). It was a Type 1 design, based closely on the Type 3 of McK&H, who exclusively supplied the NS with signalling equipment. The frame consisted of 34 levers, to a McK&H design with Hook, Cam and Soldier locking. Two arched locking room windows, with four panes across, were provided and two finials still adorned the gable ends, although the gabled porch had lost its finial. All cabins of this period (1880) were built of brick, and the upper floor window sashes, of four panes up by two across, were another standard feature.

Plate 61
Two Class 508 3-car emus Nos 508120 and 508130 approach Birkenhead Central with the 08.55 Hooton to Liverpool Loop service on 27th August 1987. Prior to arriving on the BR(LMR), these units were delivered to the BR(SR) in 1979/80. No. 508020 arrived at Strawberry Hill in December 1979 and No. 508030 was new to East Wimbledon in February 1980. Their transfer to Merseyside early in 1980, followed the arrival of Class 455 emus on the South Western Division of the BR(SR). In 1984 the Class 508s were reduced from 4 to 3-car sets and were renumbered by changing the fourth digit of the unit number from 0 to 1.

Having celebrated its centenary in 1986, the only surviving Mersey Railway cabin (out of a total of nine) is to be found at Birkenhead Central. Although there were similar features to the RSCo design, Mersey boxes were very distinctive in appearance, with stout timber corner posts, and an all-wood façade; those in the open had hipped roofs. The frame, a 27 lever RSCo design, is thought to be original. In about 1920, all the cabins were lettered, and Birkenhead Central became Cabin E.

Plate 62
On Good Friday 1982, two Class 503 3-car emus approach New Brighton with the 12.03 service from Liverpool Moorfields. The gangway doors were acquired to comply with the regulations for working in the single line Liverpool Loop which opened in May 1977. The modifications commenced in 1972, and were carried out at Horwich when the units were being serviced. The leading set (cars 28684, 29714 and 29283) is one of the batch constructed in 1938 to coincide with the extension of electrified services beyond Birkenhead Park to New Brighton and West Kirby.

The branch to New Brighton was opened just over one hundred years ago in 1888 and the RSCo was entrusted with the signalling contract. Three years later, a new company, under the Wirral Railway name, took over. Today, only four Wirral cabins remain in use (the others are Birkenhead North No. 1, No. 2 and Hoylake), and all were constructed of timber, with gable roofs. Here again, the 43 lever tappet locking frame is thought to be original. Clearly illustrated is a facing crossover road, which the train is taking; a trailing crossover, to the left of the second coach; a typical facing point layout, with facing point lock, immediately in front of the signal box; and a neat rodding run to the various points and locks.

Plate 63
Passing the delightfully named Bamber Bridge Station Level Crossing Frame on 6th August 1987, Class 47/0 No. 47159 heads 6F84, the 15.48 Blackburn to Warrington Walton Old Junction Speedlink service. The cement vehicles had originated from the Tunnel Cement Horrocksford Works, and the Cargowaggon from Fogarty's Distribution Depot. The locomotive had arrived on the 6P73 Speedlink service from Warrington and spent the intervening time as the T64 trip locomotive. On this particular day it serviced British Nuclear Fuels at Salwick and went to Blackpool North to rescue a crippled Mark III carriage.

Bamber Bridge is an interesting L&Y timber box of 1906. The horizontal boarding, rectangular 2 x 2 locking room windows, wooden staircase and operating floor windows, all standard features of this design, were as a rule prefabricated at Horwich, the principal workshops of the railway, but the cantilevered control room, provided because of space considerations at the site, and the flat roof are unusual. The twelve lever L&Y frame and gate wheel was placed at the rear. Situated on the Up East Lancashire line within the Preston PSB control area, the cabin is not now a block post, but became a gate box on 5th November 1972 to operate its own full-length MCB, installed on 11th November 1973 across the old A6 road, and, since 16th December 1973, the remote barriers at Mintholme Crossing, supervised by CCTV.

Plate 64
On 9th May 1982, Class 47/4 No. 47404 *Hadrian* (named two months earlier) heads the 09.55 (SuO) Newcastle to Liverpool service past Low Moor. This complicated diversion involved running-round at Bradford Interchange and proceeding via Dryclough, Greetland and Bradley Wood Junctions before rejoining the normal route, east of Huddersfield, at Bradley Junction. (The curve between Dryclough and Greetland Junctions and that between Bradley Wood and Bradley Junctions were closed to passenger trains in December 1986.) The locomotive was withdrawn in June 1987. It spent some time at the Tyneside Central Freight Depot but was still "rusting" at March in 1990.

L&Y box design owed much to the RSCo who built a large number of cabins (112) during the currency of their 1880's contract. So it was adopted (with minor modifications) as standard from 1899 when the L&Y established a signal works within their new Horwich complex. Built in 1893, Low Moor was absolutely typical, having segmental-arched locking room windows (a pattern directly copied from S&F) in the BTF construction, a wooden superstructure, with the "lower windows" of the sixteen sashes blanked off, horizontal boarding in the end elevations, and a hinged window in the gable. Unlike the RSCo, the L&Y fitted plain bargeboards and stovepipes instead of brick chimneys. Like the LNW however, the L&Y had standard box sizes: Low Moor was a Size 11 (notionally for 60 levers), measuring 35ft 10in in length. Box width was usually 12ft, although Low Moor was wedge-shaped, being slightly wider at the Bradford (far) end. Originally named Low Moor No. 2, and subsequently renamed Low Moor No. 2 West, it finally became plain Low Moor on 18th January 1970, when all the remaining semaphores were replaced by colour lights controlled from a panel, and Nos 1 and 5 cabins were abolished. Low Moor itself closed on 20th July 1986, when TCB working between Halifax and Mill Lane was instituted.

Plate 65
Shortly after crossing the Duddon viaduct on the approach to Foxfield, the prototype Alexander/Barclay Class 143 No. 143001 is seen en route to the Railway Technical Centre at Derby on 31st August 1985, hauled by Class 25/3 No. 25249. This section of line, opened to traffic on 1st August 1858, eliminated the reversal at Broughton which had been necessary since through running between Barrow and the Cumberland coast commenced in 1850. To the right is the former junction with the Coniston branch which closed completely on 30th April 1962.

In its early signal box design policy, the Furness Railway was more concerned to avoid styles of architecture differing with adjacent station buildings. Foxfield is therefore constructed largely of wood. Features associated with the Type 3 design, notably a steeply pitched hipped roof, and the use of Coniston stone, can clearly be seen in this rear view. Built in 1879, the box was extended in 1909 to house a new 51 lever, RSCo frame, of $5\frac{1}{2}$in pitch , although today only 14 levers are in use, and levers 25 to 43 inclusive have been removed. A closing switch is provided to enable the box to be switched out of circuit and become temporarily unmanned during slack periods of traffic while allowing the passage of trains (see Plate 38). To the right of No. 49 Down Main Second Home signal, protecting the level crossing and a trailing crossover, is Milepost $40\frac{1}{2}$ (from Carnforth), and a 20 mph PSR sign can be seen in front of the guard's van.

Plate 66
Shortly after the 13.00 Carlisle to White-haven service had cleared the section to Maryport, Class 47/3 No. 47315 approaches Aspatria with 7T57, the 12.15 Carlisle Yard to Workington trip on 6th February 1989. (As scheduled, this train had called at the British Sidac Works at Wigton for traffic purposes.)

Aspatria, now the sole representative of the Maryport & Carlisle Railway, was built around 1890 to the same design as all known 19th century M&C cabins, with a brick base, small locking room windows and a hipped roof. Many years ago, there were bay platforms at the station to serve the single line branch latterly to Mealsgate, heading off east behind the cabin, and extensive sidings opposite the box, which is situated on the Up side at the Carlisle end of the station. In 1940, a reconditioned 25 lever frame was installed, but because of wartime exigencies, this was a Horwich L&Y pattern. Today, Aspatria works AB to Maryport and Wigton and controls a trailing crossover protected by home, starting and distant signals in each direction. It too is fitted with a closing switch.

Plate 67
Before the 1986/87 timetable there was a six hour gap between Up morning trains through Annan. The new train was an extension of the 09.45 Glasgow Central to Kilmarnock service and is seen being hauled by Class 47/4 No. 47476 on 25th July 1986. Prior to May 1975, the "Thames-Clyde Express", the premier train of the day, connecting Glasgow with London St Pancras, would have been passing through. Electrification of the Nith Valley route in 1974 led to the inevitable run-down of InterCity Anglo-Scottish traffic over the former GSW main line.

One hundred years apart, nearly! The signalman's Glasgow & South Western registered car stands beside the GSW Type 1 design signal box of 1876. The vertical weather-boarding below the operating floor windows is not original, horizontal boarding being the norm when built. Originally fitted with a 23 lever frame, the cabin has had two extra levers, named A and B, added at a later date to control two remote ground frames (see Plates 179 and 180), connected to the Down Main, at Powfoot and Newbie. Annan has housed a 20 lever, Stevens frame since 1973 when colour light signals replaced the semaphores, the Down Main (in the foreground) became bi-directional, and the line to Gretna Junction was singled (work carried out under Stage 11 of the Carlisle re-signalling scheme – see Plate 201).

Plate 68
Composed of six vans, two (TOPS code) NEAs and four NKVs, on 25th July 1985, the 1S40 Euston to Stranraer parcels service, passes through Glenwhilly. This train was discontinued the following year, when the contract to carry Royal Mail parcels by rail was not renewed. As a result of its withdrawal in September 1986 this locomotive, Class 27/0 No. 27014, had the honour of being the last vacuum braked member of the class to remain in service.

Glenwhilly is one of the earliest examples of a Type 7 GSW box, with the lever frame in the back, and the stove, and typical stove-pipe at the front of the cabin. By 1905, improved visibility was the order of the day on the GSW, so the signalman's windows are much larger than those at Annan, and the locking room windows, not included in the oldest designs, are now the usual three-panes up variety. Glenwhilly is situated at a passing loop on the single line between Ayr and Stranraer Harbour, and the signalman is about to exchange the Tyers No. 6 tablet from Barrhill box for one to Dunragit box. Notice the tablet picking-up and setting-down apparatus on the Up platform in front of the third and fourth vehicles – see Plates 80 and 82.

Plate 69
Having been brought to a rest at Carmuirs East Junction, Class 37/0 No. 37110 hauls eight (TOPS code) PTA 100 tonne tipplers past Carmuirs West Junction on 14th May 1988. This service, 6S54, the 08.15(SX) Thrislington to Ravenscraig No. 4, carries dolomite for steel making. On this occasion it was running on a Saturday and boasted a 6Z54 headcode. It was likewise diverted from its normal route via Slateford Junction and Carstairs.

Although situated on the Northern Division of the Caledonian Railway, at what was once a complex network of junctions just to the south of Larbert, Carmuirs West has the low-pitched, slated roof and segmental arches formed of stretchers to the locking room windows and door associated with Southern Division Type 3 cabins. Neither the operating floor windows nor the window-cleaning walkway are original. Dating from 1882, it had a new 30 lever, Stevens frame installed in 1912 and controlled two double junctions, one from Falkirk Grahamston on which the train is travelling, and the other to Denny, since dismantled, off the left of the picture. Trailing in from the left is the line from Larbert. Notice the swing-nose crossing exactly opposite the box, set for the Grahamston direction.

Plate 70
After crossing over the Caledonian Canal on 4th June 1988, Class 37/4 No. 37414 accelerates past Clachnaharry with the 18.20 Inverness to Kyle of Lochalsh service. In the distance is the Kessock Bridge which carries the A9 road over the Moray Firth. In 1985, Chris Green – then General Manager of the Scottish Region – stated that BR was struggling to recover the 15% business lost since the new bridge was constructed. Ironically, during the period between the collapse of the Waterloo Bridge on 7th February 1989 and the opening of the new structure on 14th May 1990, it was the road bridge which provided a fast link with Dingwall to connect with the severed rail service to the north!

Clachnaharry is a timber McK&H Type 3/Highland Railway design, built in 1912, and is a fairly rare example of a single line token station with no loops or sidings. Since singling of the double track westwards to Clunes in 1966, Clachnaharry has controlled only the swing bridge over the Caledonian Canal and its protecting signals. Before Inverness Signalling Centre (see Plate 209) was commissioned, the Inverness–Clachnaharry single line section was worked by No. 6 Tyers tablet machines; from 21st March 1987 it was worked by TCB (Single Line) regulations. The driver is collecting the key token for the single line to Muir of Ord, which today is worked from Inverness Signalling Centre by the RETB system (see Plates 85 to 87).

Plate 71

The 9B91 trip from Ogmore Vale Washery composed of a rake of empty high capacity coal wagons (TOPS code) MDVs is propelled by Class 37/0 No. 37234 into the sidings at Tondu Middle Junction on 15th April 1982. The Ogmore Washery and the line (diverging to the right) have since closed, and the only remaining traffic beyond Tondu uses the Maesteg route to Llynfi Junction. The open land to the right was formerly the site of the steam depot (shed code 88H).

Opened in 1886, Tondu Middle, was built as a GW Type 3 cabin but has since been considerably modified. Originally, it would have had large segmental arched locking room windows and vertical boarding between the operating floor string course and the windows. These too have been altered and would have been of the three panes deep variety (seen in Plate 74). The gabled roof and small curved eaves brackets are however typical of this design. Situated at what was once an important intersection of four routes – three single line and one double track – Tondu is equipped with a 65 lever GW frame, installed in 1963.

Plate 72

After leaving the much diminished yard at Rood End (beyond the bridge), Class 25/3 No. 25313 approaches Langley Green on 20th August 1985 with a short 6T48 trip working to Albright & Wilson's factory, located on the former Oldbury branch. The train is composed of a barrier wagon and four ICI (Mond Division) chlorine tanks.

A completely new departure in GW box design appeared in 1896 with the Type 7. Perhaps the most striking feature was the new style operating floor windows with fewer glazing bars (3-up, 2-down pattern), in sliding sashes, except the centre bay, to improve the signalman's view. Bright red bricks, with specially shaped ones for the segmental arched locking room windows, large decorative eaves brackets and a hipped roof, originally used on Type 2 cabins, were the hallmarks of this design, which was destined to become familiar throughout the system. Of the many still in use today, Langley Green represents Type 7b, with ridge tiles replacing the finials and lead flashing of Type 7a. Measuring 38ft by 13ft by 7ft 6in, and mounted on the northern end of the Up platform, it opened in 1904 as Langley Green Middle. With the closure on 29th April 1979 of the West box, whose level crossing it today supervises by CCTV, it became plain Langley Green and works AB to Smethwick Junction (right) and Rowley Regis.

Plate 73
Class 45/0 No. 45029 propels three (TOPS code) VDA vans past Kingswinford Junction on 28th August 1985. The train is the 6T42 trip from Shut End to Brierley Hill Steel Terminal. The 1½ mile Shut End (Pensnett) branch (diverging to the left above the locomotive) is all that remains of the Kingswinford branch to Oxley Branch Junction (Wolverhampton).

Introduced at the same time as the GW Type 7, the Type 27 was a similar standardised design, except built of timber, with horizontal weatherboarding. The main difference however was the locking room windows with the conventional and common 4-panes wide by 3-panes deep sashes. During its 30 years' life, this design changed little: brick chimneys, lead flashing and finials were superseded by stove-pipes, ridge tiles and hip-hooks, as seen at Kingswinford Junction South (Type 27c). With a 77 lever, 3-bar vertical tappet frame, of 1924, it works AB to Eagle Crossing (right) and Stourbridge Junction.

Plate 74
Two Class 150/1 'Sprinter' units, led by No. 150141, drift into Tywyn with the 16.37 Machynlleth to Pwllheli train on 1st August 1987. This station became the terminus of Cambrian services when damage by worms resulted in the complete closure of the Barmouth Bridge in 1980. After much speculation, the bridge reopened in May 1981 and through trains recommenced. Loco-hauled workings were excluded until repairs were completed in May 1986.

The first standardised GW box design, conceived for system-wide use, was the brick Type 5 (itself a derivative of the earlier Type 4). From it, the decidedly rare timber Type 25, illustrated here, was developed. Built mainly from 1889 to 1897, it had a gable roof, with the familiar 4-louvre gable vents and "rocket" ridge vents. Multi-pane windows, in sliding sashes in every bay were common, but the GW never provided a window cleaning walkway as standard on any box. Originally, the main corner posts and horizontal waistband at operating floor level were painted brown. Reincarnated in 1923 from the structure formerly at Maidenhead East, Tywyn, before its closure in 1988, contained a 38 lever GW frame, working EKT regulations (see Plate 82) to Dovey Junction (see Plate 196) and Barmouth South (see Plate 44).

Plate 75
Prior to taking the Vale of Glamorgan line at Barry, Class 37/0s No 37224 and 37205 slow for a crew change while heading the 7C92 Taff Merthyr to Aberthaw mgr working on 6th August 1986. Slow-speed control Class 47/3 No. 47325 replaced the Class 37s at Aberthaw for the journey through the power station unloader. In January 1987, single Class 37/7s replaced pairs of Class 37/0s and there is no longer a change of locomotive in the Exchange Sidings.

The Barry Railway employed contractors for the construction of signal boxes and the famous firm of EOD built the Barry Type 1 cabin at Barry station and supplied the original lever frame about 1897. Similar to the GE Type 5, this design – the only surviving example – shared common features such as the bargeboard decoration, the "rusticated" woodwork in the gable ends, and the sub-division of the upper panes of the operating floor windows into four. The verandah however is not a standard feature. Situated at the Cardiff end of the Down platform, Barry today contains a 77 lever GW frame, installed in the rear of the box in 1957. It works to fringe cabins at Barry Island, Aberthaw (East) – the sole representative of the Barry Type 2 design – and Cardiff PSB.

Plate 76
On 14th April 1982, Class 37/0 No. 37210 passes through Taffs Well station with a Stormstown to Ocean trip working composed of 22 loaded mineral (TOPS code) MDV wagons. The route to Aber Junction diverges to the right. This line was "mothballed" in June 1982 and closed at the end of the same year. The track was lifted in 1984 when it was clear that Cardiff Queen Street could handle the remaining coal traffic originating in the Rhymney Valley.

Introduced from around 1895, in both timber and brick varieties, the Taff Vale Type box was less ornate than its predecessor, the McK&H Type 3, whose contours it closely followed. The terracotta finials and cockscomb ridge tiles gave way to timber finials and plain ridge tiles, but the decoration of the fascia boards and the bargeboards survived. The wooden superstructure of the BTF examples included weatherboarding with vents in the gable ends, and a porch. Sited at the Cardiff end of the Up platform at Taffs Well station, with the formation of the Goods lines behind it, the confusingly named Walnut Tree Junction box controls the line to Aber Junction (right), the single line branch to Nantgarw (diverging right beyond the Down platform), and the main to Pontypridd. To the left of No. 4 Down Main Starting (at clear) is No. 5 Down Main to Down Goods Starting.

Plate 77
On 1st August 1987, Class 37/4 No. 37427 *Pont y Bermo* passes slowly through Caersws while heading the 08.00 (SO) Pwllheli to Euston "Snowdonian" service. The late Brian Haresnape described this delightful rural station as "... a classic example of an elderly building which is thoroughly acceptable to today's travellers". The cabin survived into 1990 to control the gates.

Because of its failure to provide adequately interlocked cabins before the 1889 Regulation of Railways Act made block working and interlocking, inter alia, compulsory, the impecunious Cambrian Railways was forced to embark on a grand catching-up exercise in the early 1890s. Dating from 1891, Caersws was built by Dutton & Co. Ltd to their Type 1, a design closely resembling the McK&H Type 3. On a BTF base, the superstructure consists of $6\frac{1}{4}$in lapped boarding, surrounding 2 x 3 panes windows, decorated bargeboards and finials, and a brick chimney. With its original 18 lever Dutton frame, Caersws was situated at the Shrewsbury end of the bi-directional Up and Down Main, 53 miles 31 chains from Sutton Bridge Junction (see Plate 230). It worked EKT regulations to Talerddig (see Plate 80) and Newtown, until the Machynlleth RETB scheme superseded these boxes on 21st October 1988. Although the Up and Down Loop (left foreground) had been lifted on 11th January 1987, No. 16 Up Main Second Home signal and distant were still positioned on the "wrong" side of the line.

Plate 78
The "North and West" route lost its InterCity status in 1970 when the remaining services from Liverpool/Manchester to South Wales/West Country were diverted via Birmingham. In May 1988, after nearly two decades of decline the Provincial sector demonstrated its confidence in the route by doubling the frequency of the service and the introduction of 'Super-Sprinters' coincided in May 1988. However, two locomotive-hauled diagrams were retained to cover the short-fall in the delivery of Class 155 sets. On 4th August 1988, Class 37/4 No. 37427 *Pont y Bermo* speeds through Leominster with the 13.23 Cardiff Central to Liverpool Lime Street train.

The early signal cabins of the Shrewsbury and Hereford – part of the LNW/GW Joint Lines – were very standardised. Built probably by the railway company itself around 1875, to control a level crossing, which was removed and replaced by an overbridge a few years later, Leominster is a Type 1 design, based on the S&F Type 1, but with the distinguishing features of a string course at operating floor level and a splay stone course immediately below the upper floor windows. Constructed on a brick plinth (see Plate 124), like many early cabins, Leominster (formerly the South box) is almost square in plan, (roughly 15ft), and had an attractive finial surmounting the hipped roof. With segmental arches to the cast iron locking room windows in both front and end elevations, it remains to control the Down Sidings and supervise AHB at Leominster Crossing, 1,279 yards to the north. It works AB to Woofferton and Moreton-on-Lugg.

4 : Single Line Working

Plate 79
Considering passenger services were discontinued over 30 years ago, the platform and associated buildings at Ammanford are in excellent condition. On 8th August 1986, Class 37/0 No. 37308 heads 9F36 Pantyffynnon New Sidings to Abernant Colliery trip along the Garnant Valley. The wagons are a mixture of fitted (TOPS code) MDV and unfitted MDO 21 tonne types. (Out of sight at the rear of the train, was Class 37/5 No. 37505, transferred shortly afterwards from Canton to Thornaby.) Much traffic that previously used the now closed Wernos Washery is sent to Abernant for washing. The track in the foreground connects the nearby Betws Drift (right) with Pantyffynnon.

Bi-directional single lines are worked on the principle of preventing more than one train being in a block section between two boxes at the same time. To achieve this objective, a number of methods have been evolved over the last 120 years or so, each new one being an improvement in terms of reliability and versatility over previous methods. One of the simplest forms of SLW, generally confined to cul-de-sac branch lines, uses a single authority, known as a train staff, consisting of a length of wood or metal, engraved with the name of the branch or the two locations between which it applies. The crew must be in possession of the staff before they can proceed onto the single line and must return it to the signalman before another train is allowed to enter that section. Originally termed 'One Engine in Steam' working, and now more prosaically called 'One Train Working', this system is both cheap to operate in terms of signal engineering and widely used on BR today.

Plate 80
With power to spare, Class 37/4 No. 37430 *Cwmbran* breasts Talerddig Summit heading the 10.15 (SO) Aberystwyth to Euston express on 1st August 1987. The locomotive was named to commemorate the reopening of the station serving the New Town near the southern end of the "North and West" route. The ceremony took place on 11th May 1986 and normal passenger services commenced the following day.

Strict instructions regarding the receipt and delivery of Electric Token apparatus used to appear with diagrams in Table D1 of the various BR Sectional Appendices (available for sale at Collectors' Corner, Euston). Nowadays, the most common ways of effecting a token exchange are by hand, as at Ammanford, or by using fixed lineside equipment, consisting of a token receiver and a token deliverer. This is provided at some cabins to speed up the exchange procedure, and the driver, on the bi-directionally signalled Up and Down line at Talerddig, no doubt obeying the mandatory 15mph speed restriction when carrying out this exchange(!), has just set down the Machynlleth–Talerddig token on the receiving post, situated 16 yards after passing the box, (adjacent to the rear cab of the locomotive), and is about to pick up the Talerddig–Caersws token from the delivering post, 37 yards beyond the cabin. Being rather small and to prevent accidental damage or loss, the tokens themselves are fixed in a carrier, to which is attached a large metal hoop. This enables the driver to pass the hoop over the projecting arm of the "setting down" post, and to catch the new token by passing his forearm through the hoop of the token carrier on the "picking up" post. Note the paraffin oil lamps to illuminate the apparatus at night, and also the run-off siding for the lengthman's trolley.

Plate 81
An afternoon movement from Sunderland South Dock to Murton Colliery on 5th March 1984 approaches Murton Crossing on the freight-only route from Ryhope Grange. Considering the continuous climb, much at 1 in 44, Class 37/0 No. 37283 is making easy going with a rake of empty (TOPS code) HTV hoppers. After loading with colliery waste, the train departed for Seaham Harbour via Sunderland South Dock for running-round. (Note the continuous welded track which had been laid on both lines of the 5 mile 69 chain branch in the summer of 1980.)

No train staff is provided, and movements are agreed by telephone between the operators at each end of the section where OTW without Train Staff regulations apply. A lightly-trafficked single line, such as the South Hetton branch, is an example. Here, on 29th January 1984, the former Down Branch became the new bi-directional single line between Ryhope Grange and Hawthorn Combined Mine & Coke Plant and the intermediate cabins at Seaton and Murton were reduced to gate box status. Both were subsequently abolished, (Murton on 13th May 1984) and each level crossing was converted to AOCL (see Plate 134). When this photograph was taken, the Up Branch was awaiting recovery while No. 1, the former Up Home signal, motor-operated from a small IFS panel in the box, applied to the new single line. Murton was a NE Type N2 design – compare with Usworth (Plate 111).

Plate 82
Coming off the single line section from Melton, Class 105 dmu (cars 51290 and 54431) arrives at Saxmundham with the 17.40 Ipswich to Lowestoft service on 17th April 1984. The next Down working was the 16.50 Liverpool Street to Lowestoft, headed by Class 47/4 No. 47544. The following month the through train from London was discontinued, leaving the East Suffolk line with no regular locomotive hauled passenger services. (Note the former Down line was still in situ but had been out of use for nine months.)

The most common method of SLW is the EKT Block system (see Plate 80) which can be sub-divided into the Staff, Tablet and Token systems, each using apparatus of different appearance but with the same purpose. It employs a set of (usually 24 or 30) identically engraved and serially numbered authorities, which are electrically interlocked in compatible instruments (or machines) at the cabins of the block sections to which they refer. Co-operative effort is required of the two signalmen to release one of these authorities; until its replacement in one or other of the machines, no further authority can be obtained. To obviate the risk of a token being accidentally inserted by the signalman in the wrong instrument for an adjacent single line section, different lock configurations are provided for each set of staffs, tablets or tokens. Entering Saxmundham on the bi-directional Up line, the driver of this Down train is about to surrender the Woodbridge–Saxmundham token, while the signalman is busy closing the gates of Rendham Road level crossing, six chains to the south, where the former movable Up platform was situated. A GE Type 2 box, Saxmundham is now the control centre for the RETB signalling on the East Suffolk line and the Sizewell branch (see Plates 88, 89 and 90).

Plate 83
On 21st August 1984, the 13.00 Oban to Glasgow Queen Street train comes off the short connection between the former Caledonian and North British routes at Crianlarich. It was only after the closure of the Caledonian line east of Crianlarich (Lower) in 1965, that the regular Oban services were diverted to use the West Highland line south of Crianlarich and terminated at Queen Street and not the former Buchanan Street station. Class 37/0 No. 37081 *Loch Long* has since been renumbered No. 37797 and in August 1986 the name was transferred to No. 37407.

Introduced from the late 1960s on the BR(ScR) (and elsewhere on BR to a lesser extent), Tokenless Block (TB) working, as its name implies, is a development of the EKT Block system, but without a physical token. The main features are a short track circuit at each end of the single line section, with a treadle at the exit end, and electrically connected block instruments, (on

the ScR, similar in appearance and operation to existing token machines), which release the starting signals on acceptance of a train for one train only. At the time this photograph was taken, the Oban branch (left) was worked (as the sign indicates) by the EKT regulations, but the main line towards Fort William (behind the first coach) was a TB section to the then named Tyndrum Upper. No. 21 Down Main Starting to Fort William – the taller arm of this double invisible lattice post left-hand bracket signal (see Plate 93) applies through No. 16 facing crossover (below the first coach), while No. 20 signal is released by the withdrawal of the key token from the Crianlarich – Dalmally EKT instrument. The train has passed No. 19 Up Branch Second Home signal (above the last coach) and is entering the Up Main Platform via No. 13 facing crossover.

Plate 84
After languishing at Carlisle for nearly two years, Class 40 No. 40122 was moved to Toton in May 1983 for renovation and repainting in original green livery. The first train hauled by the 'revitalised' No. D200 was the 08.48 King's Cross to Carlisle "Hadrian Pullman" on 31st July 1983. It is seen running-round at Warcop, having traversed all that remains of the former NE trans-Pennine route via Stainmore. The route closed to through traffic in 1962 and freight services to Warcop were discontinued in March 1989.

Latterly the 6½ mile Warcop branch was governed by the OTW regulations from Appleby as far as the notice board, beyond which Shunting Area instructions were in force. As the name suggests, train crews were at liberty within the siding area to do more or less what they wanted in terms of shunting, etc., although of course when special passenger trains were run on the branch, much stricter operating procedures applied. On the former NE Eden Valley branch, the box, a small Central Division Type C2a (see Plate 110), replaced its 1876 predecessor in 1912, although quite why this design was used at that date – especially since the Central Division had been abolished in 1899 – is unclear! (Can anyone help the authors, via the publishers please?) Its 15 lever, Stevens frame remained in situ until recently. Note the NE standard style, though not original, diagonal fencing.

Plate 85
ScotRail's last vacuum braked passenger service, the "Royal Scotsman", is arguably its most prestigious! In 1988, from 17th May until 25th October, the service departed from Edinburgh each Tuesday and returned the following Sunday. The itinerary included Oban, Fort William, Aviemore, Kyle of Lochalsh and Inverness. On the fourth day after stabling overnight, 1Z98 the 06.40 Plockton to Inverness service approaches Dingwall on 4th June 1988 headed by Class 37/4 No. 37414. The day concluded when the train was stabled overnight at the head of the Dufftown branch at Keith.

Signalling in transition. When photographed, Dingwall North's No. 10 Down Main to Kyle Branch Starting (lower arm) and No. 9 Down Main Starting (to Wick/Thurso) were the most northerly Down signals in Scotland, governing access to two routes controlled by RETB from a new block post on the Down platform of Dingwall station. Developed in response to the need for a low-cost but highly reliable signalling system with the same order of integrity as that provided by existing methods, RETB satisfies the requirements for signalling lightly-trafficked single or double track railways, making use of two existing developments, radio communication and computer-based interlocking, to create a high technology alternative.

Plate 86
The Beeching Report recommended closure of all routes north of Inverness. However, the construction of the aluminium smelter at Invergordon and the exploitation of North Sea oil helped to save the Far North Line while the Kyle of Lochalsh route lacked any industrial development. After a decade of uncertainty, the immediate threat to the line was lifted on 31st July 1974, following the passing of the 1974 Railways Act. (The other routes reprieved were: Stockport to Stalybridge, the Cambrian Coast, Bedford to Bletchley, Wimbledon to West Croydon and Ashford to Hastings.) This 4th June 1988 view depicts Class 37/4 No. 37421 after leaving the Kyle line at Dingwall while heading the 11.28 service to Inverness.

The first part of the modernisation was commissioned in August 1979 when speech communication between trains and block posts was established by radio and landline via Inverness. Radio communication between signal cabins on the Far North Line followed on 1st August 1980. The recent rapid evolution of mobile radio systems and microprocessors has made available the technology necessary for RETB, i.e. radio interface hardware and a specially adapted computer (or SSI), with an inbuilt safety and security system equal to earlier single line methods. To implement RETB, trains using the line must be fitted with radio telephones, aerials (see Plate 89) and special in-cab "Token Display" units. The first installation of RETB (between Dingwall and Kyle of Lochalsh – a distance of some 63 miles) was brought into use for a six month experimental trial on 6th July 1984.

Plate 87
Framed by Polybulk wagons which had arrived on the 6H33 trip working from Inverness the previous day, Class 37/4 No. 37417 *Highland Region* heads the 10.10 Inverness to Kyle of Lochalsh "Hebridean Heritage" service on 4th June 1988. Note the observation car at the rear which was converted from Class 101 trailer car No. 54356 in 1987 and repainted in the green/cream livery the following year. (In the 1960s an observation car from the short-lived "Devon Belle" Pullman train was used. In those days full vision was obtained on both the outward and return journeys by use of the locomotive turntable at Kyle!)

At Muir of Ord, the removal of semaphore signalling and the provision of train-operated points and associated "Points Set" indicators (see Plate 89) with new reflectorised Stop and Distant boards, and Station Limits markers, was carried out in January 1988. This preparatory work for the commissioning (on 28th August 1988) of the 18 mile RETB "missing link" between Inverness and Dingwall also saw the inauguration of right-hand running through the station. The £200,000 scheme resulted in the closure of Dingwall station RETB centre, Muir of Ord box, the ground frames at Dingwall North and South (former cabins), and the reduction of Clachnaharry to swing bridge box status. Nearly 250 miles of railway from Inverness to Kyle of Lochalsh, Wick and Thurso are now controlled by the RETB signalman in Inverness Signalling Centre (see Plate 209).

Plate 88
Nowadays at Westerfield, all Up East Suffolk and both Up and Down Felixstowe services use the Up platform while the Down is only used by Down East Suffolk trains. In this 25th August 1988 illustration, the 12.25 Ipswich to Felixstowe service is formed from 3-car Class 101 dmu (cars 53305, 59536 and 53321). (Yes, the story had a happy ending; the lady, the children and the dog, having arrived at the last minute on the wrong platform, did catch the train!)

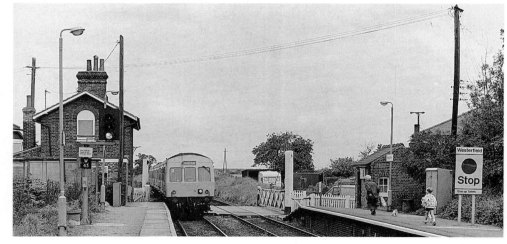

RETB may be used on either single or double lines of railway, or a combination of both, the Ipswich to Lowestoft branch being a good example of the last. Controlled from Saxmundham box, RETB was brought into use on 16th February 1986, when Melton, Halesworth and Beccles (South) cabins were closed, and all existing signalling between Westerfield Junction and Oulton Broad North (both exclusive) was abolished. The RETB sections are: Westerfield Junction–Woodbridge (double line section); Woodbridge–Saxmundham; Saxmundham–Halesworth (double line section); Halesworth–Oulton Broad South; Saxmundham–Siding; Saxmundham–Branch (Saxmundham Junction); Branch (Saxmundham Junction)–Sizewell. Each location is a Token Exchange point.

Plate 89
Since the withdrawal of the ubiquitous Cravens dmus from East Anglia, the area has been inundated by Class 101 sets displaced from their previous duties by 'Sprinters' and 'Pacers'. The only complete Class 104 2-car passenger set to survive this purge was the green liveried set (cars 53359 and 54122). It was specially treated by Stratford works early in 1986, and after a short period operating out of Stratford depot, was transferred to Norwich Crown Point. On 30th August 1988, it is seen at Oulton Broad North only weeks before withdrawal. Despite its imminent demise, it had managed to clip five minutes off the schedule of the 09.50 Norwich to Lowestoft fast service!

Concurrently with the development of RETB, an associated project for the automation of points at passing loops or elsewhere was being progressed by the Director of BRB S&T Engineering. Eliminating the need for signalmen at intermediate places, and thereby reducing staff costs considerably, this apparatus, consisting of a hydro-pneumatic, train-operated, self-normalising points mechanism, automatically sets and detects the points in the normal position for facing moves from say, a single to double track section, as on the Up approach to Halesworth station, and also operates like a pair of spring points for trailing movements. Located between 50 and 100 yards on the approach to the facing points, through which a 15 mph PSR is in force, a "Points Set" indicator (a steady yellow light) confirms the lie of the points to the driver. When photographed, those at the north end of Dingwall station (Plate 85) had not been commissioned. Note the radio aerial at Oulton Broad North box, a GE Type 7 structure.

Plate 90
On 30th August 1988, Norwich based 3-car Class 101 dmu (cars 53149, 59077 and 53170) enters Oulton Broad South with the 09.20 Ipswich to Lowestoft train. Of the nine sets originally fitted with radio receivers in 1985, this is one of the four that remain in service. The section of the East Suffolk Line between Oulton Broad North and Halesworth was singled in September 1985 and all traffic concentrated on the former Up platform at Oulton Broad South.

In RETB areas, various types of notice boards take the place of conventional signals. Here, at the London end of Oulton Broad South station, is an End of Section marker board (the equivalent of a starting (or section) signal in semaphore signalling), with below, a Radio Channel Change Board. This is a black oval displaying a white reflective diamond on which the channel number is shown in black. The other four Radio Channel Change boards are placed at Westerfield Junction, Wickham Market, Brampton and Beccles. In the event of a failure of radio communication, five emergency telephones communicating with Saxmundham box are provided at various locations. Station Limit Boards (not shown), consisting of a vertically mounted white rectangle with diagonal blue stripes, are placed roughly 200 to 300 yards beyond each End of Section board. On passing this marker board, a driver reports to the signalman that the station is clear for the following train.

Plate 91
On 6th February 1986 Class 56 No. 56088 accelerates past Pelaw with a mgr working from Swalwell Opencast Concentration Depot to Tyne Dock. (The Tyne Coal Terminal was opened on 7th November 1985 as a joint venture between the Port of Tyne Authority, British Coal and BR.) The Class 56s arrived on Tyneside in 1981, gradually replacing the Class 37s that had enjoyed a virtual monopoly on coal workings since the end of steam traction in 1967.

Reversible road working (today more commonly referred to as bi-directional signalling) where a line or series of lines is fitted with fixed signals governing movements in either direction for use at any time, is increasingly being employed as a means to boost line capacity and/or to reduce the amount of expensive fixed equipment needed to provide the facilities required for moving the trains. Between Pelaw and Gateshead, the Tyne & Wear Metro poached the BR passenger lines (southern pair, left) leaving the two Goods lines to accommodate all BR traffic. Hence, two-way signalling over the Down and Up Pelaw (former Goods) lines, controlled from Gateshead PSB, was introduced on 31st May 1981, worked by TCB double line regulations in each direction. A 30 mph PSR is imposed on the Pelaw lines in the reverse direction. Note the wide-to-gauge trap points on the Down Pelaw Goods Loop, adjacent to G45 signal, to protect the Down Pelaw Main.

Plate 92
On the day of the 1982 Flower Festival, three Class 114 2-car dmu sets (cars 50039 and 56001, 56049 and 50033, 50012 and 56043), await departure from Spalding with 1G43, the 16.43 to Peterborough relief service, while alongside, Class 31/1 No. 31130 heads 1Z79, the 16.35 Bicester return excursion. (The 50xxx and 56xxx units have since been renumbered in the 53xxx and 54xxx series.)

Both-way signalling is not a new development, but it is only in the last two decades or so that its full potential has been exploited. A nostalgic look back at the Up side of Spalding station shows a dmu on the Up Joint line, protected by No. 14 signal on the "wrong" side of the line, and a Class 31 waiting at No. 10 Up Main Home signal, with No. 5 Up Bay Platform Home on the extreme right. Resignalling arrived on 22nd July 1984, when Spalding No. 2 box (at the Sleaford end of the Up Joint platform – left of the photograph) was closed and a simplified track layout controlled by a mixture of 2 and 3-aspect colour lights from a small IFS panel in Spalding No. 1 cabin (renamed Spalding) was commissioned. The Up Main became a bi-directional line between a facing crossover south of Spalding (Winsover Road) MCB level crossing, and a trailing crossover just north of the station, and the Up Joint became the Down Main. TCB is worked from Spalding to Mill Green box, some $\frac{3}{4}$ mile away on the Sleaford side of the station.

5 : Signalling Materials

Plate 93
Drawing out of Reedham station, a Class 105 dmu (cars 51293 and 54131) forms the 09.49 Norwich to Yarmouth service on 17th April 1984. At Reedham Junction, it will take the stretch to Breydon Junction, where this route, and that via Acle, run as two parallel single lines into the former Vauxhall station. The seven mile connection, via Berney Arms, is protected until 1992 when a five year support deal with Norfolk County Council expires.

Several different materials, principally wood, metal and reinforced concrete, were used in the construction of semaphore signals, and lattice steel (again, there were three main varieties of pattern), used widely by McK&H and Stevens among others, was common at the turn of the century. Often the actual signal dolls were built of lattice steel too (see Plate 85) but at Reedham, No. 53 Up Main Second Home signal now has a wooden doll with LNER flat cap finial. Dating from June 1904, when the line to Reedham Swing Bridge was doubled and a new cabin (to the right, behind the photographer) was provided, this flat-braced lattice steel right-hand bracket was constructed in a difficult position over the Up Sidings and on the "wrong" side of the box, to improve the driver's view of it.

Plate 94
Before 1984 the basic service between Ashford and Canterbury West was composed of two trains in each direction per hour: the fast trains from Charing Cross, and as depicted here, the stopping service from Victoria to Ramsgate/Margate. Today, the basic service is hourly and, since 1986, combines at Ashford with the portion that has travelled via Dover, before proceeding to Charing Cross via Tonbridge. Trains for Victoria (via Maidstone East) are limited to peak periods. Approaching Wye on 23rd August 1983, the 16.52 Ramsgate to Victoria working is formed from Class 423 (4-VEP) emu No. 7867 (since renumbered No. 3167).

The three elements of the SR's drive for economy in the early 1930s, because of the increasing road transport competition, are illustrated here: the extension of third-rail electrification; the wide-spread use of concrete, to supply virtually everything from lamp standards, lineside huts, and sectional footbridges; and the introduction of scrap rail for the cheap construction of signal posts – an ingenious solution! Straight post signals, such as No. 5 Down Main Starting at Wye, were invariably constructed of two bull-head rails bolted together. Gantries, right and left hand brackets, and suspended doll brackets used four rails to carry the extra weight. The posts were easily assembled and so extremely strong and durable that the BR(SR) perpetuated this successful idea until the late 1960s, when the tubular-steel post was adopted as standard.

Plate 95
Prior to halting for a crew change on platform 1 at Exeter St David's station, Class 47/0 No. 47143 approaches Red Cow level crossing with an excursion from Worcester to Paignton on 9th August 1984. On the right, Class 33/1 No. 33112 is stabled at Waterloo Road at the head of the 6B45 Meldon Quarry to Exeter Riverside ballast working.

Tubular steel was another common material used by all companies particularly from the 1930s onwards. This imposing bracket signal, with tubular steel dolls and a 10 inch diameter main stem, stood guarding the eastern approach to St David's station until it was replaced on 31st March 1985 by the colour-light seen in the background. It admitted trains to the Down Bay platform (right-hand doll), the Down Main (platform 1), the Down

Main (a through line – tallest post) and the Down Middle (platform 3). All the routes have calling-on signals, and all the through routes have distant arms, belonging to Exeter West box: the Down Middle arm (left) is fixed, while the Down Main is motor-worked.

Plate 96
Class 47/4 No. 47401 *North Eastern* and Class 31/4 No. 31450 head 6E69, the 11.45 (SO) Langley Oil Terminal to Humber Oil Refinery service on 23rd May 1987. It is seen at West Holmes (Lincoln), passing the trackbed that led to the former Great Central West Goods depot. At the time *North Eastern* was one of the dedicated fleet of Class 47/4s for use on the Provincial sector's Trans-Pennine services! With the closure of Gateshead depot in May 1988, No. 47401 was reallocated to Immingham and the name was transferred to Class 47/4 No. 47443.

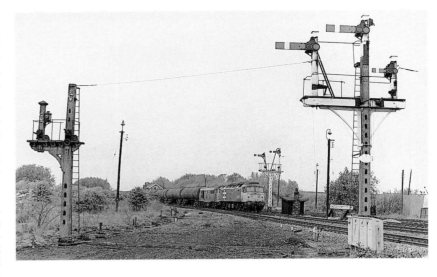

Pioneered by the M&GN at their Melton Constable works, concrete signal posts were introduced by a number of other railway companies, notably the CLC, GC, GN, GW and LBSC. They were heavier for a given size, and cheaper, but were brittle and difficult to handle, having to be made to a carefully designed template with all the pear-shaped holes pre-positioned, so that the necessary fittings could be bolted through later. This photograph shows the former No. 2 and No. 3 signals on the concrete left-hand bracket at West Holmes, and the Down Main Home boards, to Boultham Junction (No. 18, left doll), to East Holmes (No. 28), and the miniature arm No. 38 signal to the both-way signalled Transfer Line, all sited 206 yards from the cabin.

Plate 97
Class 47/0 No. 47191 accelerates out of Ely with the 10.06 Kings Lynn to Liverpool Street service on 16th April 1984. (No. 47191 was withdrawn in July 1987 and it was still languishing at Springs Branch depot at the beginning of 1990.) These services remained in the hands of steam heated locomotives until May 1984 and, prior to 1983, the diagrams were shared between Class 47/0s and Class 37/0s. Diesel hauled trains on the Anglia section of Network SouthEast ceased in May 1990, over a year before the £20.1 million electrification scheme was due to be completed between Cambridge and Kings Lynn in October 1991.

What an amazing assortment of signal structures live on at Ely Dock Junction! The concrete post left-hand bracket controls movements on the Down Goods Loop, while the tubular steel bracket refers to the Down Main. The lattice steel balanced bracket applies from the Down Branch (Soham cabin), while a 4-way tubular steel shunting signal presides over moves from the Up Main. No. 25 Up Main Intermediate Block Distant signal (see Plate 177), protruding from the box, was abolished on 3rd February 1985, when preliminary work to link up Ely Dock Junction with Cambridge PSB was undertaken.

6 : Pre-Grouping (LNER & SR) Signal Boxes

All is at rest at the Lincolnshire resort of Skegness during the afternoon of 27th July 1981. Closest to the camera is the 18.40 (FSX) service to Burton-on-Trent headed by Class 20s Nos 20068 and 20073. Class 40 No. 40069 is on the 18.33 return excursion to Newcastle-upon-Tyne. On the right, two more Class 20s, Nos 20186 and 20188 are attached to the 18.53 (FSX) train for Leicester. Close scrutiny will reveal Class 31/1 No. 31315 – wedged between the signal box and the Class 20s – forming the 17.20 working for Sheffield.

On the GN, there was no real attempt at standardisation of box design until about 1888. However, almost all the early cabins had gabled, steeply-pitched roofs, with large finials and ornamental bargeboards. Situated at the London end of platforms 3/4 and built in 1883, Skegness is one of the few timber Type 1 boxes, with the characteristic vents in the gable end. These were more often fitted horizontally and varied between 2 and 5 panes across. The original nameboard has been removed. In 1900, a new RSCo 80 lever frame (with 4in centres) was installed, but today, with extensive track abandonments, particularly of the stabling sidings on the south (right-hand) side, about half the levers are spares.

Approaching Sykes Junction, Class 31/4 No. 31468 heads the 09.20(SO) Leeds to Skegness train on 23rd May 1987. This was formerly the meeting place between the 'Joint' line and the Great Central route to Clarborough Junction. When the latter ceased to be a through route on 2nd November 1959, traffic was diverted via Gainsborough. The stub from Clarborough Junction was subsequently used for access to Cottam Power Station, while the section from Sykes Junction was reduced to a single line to service the crude oil terminal at Torksey. The branch and cabin were closed in September 1988, shortly after the closure of the Torksey terminal.

When the only suitable site for a signal box was on the side of an embankment, many companies frequently resorted to timber as the medium of construction. The GN Type 2 design, represented here by Sykes Junction, of 1885, was rather plain, with weather-boarding, a low-pitched roof, and ubiquitous vent in the gable end. Housing a McK&H 18 lever frame, Sykes Junction was switched out when photographed. Notice the illuminated 'T' sign – an indication to drivers of the termination of a temporary speed restriction; the horse-shoe above the door, an unofficial though common embellishment; and, in the field, a new breed of quadruped – of the equivocal, bi-directional species!

Plate 100
Early in 1972 the Total oil company established a new railhead on the site of the former GN marshalling yard at Colwick. A train from this terminal, 7E38 the 09.58 Rectory Junction to Lindsey Oil Refinery, hauled by Class 56 No. 56085, is seen at Lowfield on 31st July 1984. The last freight train over the section between Bottesford West Junction and Newark ran on 16th April 1987.

Although built four years after Skegness, Lowfield was the brick equivalent of Type 1. Vertical boarding in the gable end and the horizontal vent, since boarded up, were common features. The lean, slim-looking windows, too, were typical, extending about 18in above operating floor level up to the eaves. Only five levers of the 30 lever RSCo frame, of 1900, were in use at this time. The train has just left the single line section from Bottesford West and the signalman has just collected the hooped pouch containing the single line token. The line and therefore the cabin closed in April 1987.

Plate 101
Derby Suburban Class 115 dmu – composed of cars 51670, 59661, 59664 and 51660 – restarts the 14.40 Aylesbury to Marylebone train out of Great Missenden on Good Friday, 1984. Earlier the same year, BR announced their intention to close the London terminus by allowing London Regional Transport to operate these services into Baker Street. Banbury/Princes Risborough trains were to be diverted into Paddington. After two years of uncertainty, it was reprieved when LT indicated they would not be able to cope with the increased demand.

Based on the S&F Type 5 design, all Metropolitan Railway Type 1 boxes were constructed of timber, with brick chimneys; Great Missenden is an 1892 example. The decorative wood panelled features seen in this end elevation were replicated on the box front, where a locking room window was fitted, in the centre, below the horizontal waist band. In each window bay, except the front centre, there was one sliding and one fixed sash, each of two panes deep. The cabin houses an original 30 lever, tappet locking frame, variously described as Metropolitan, but having some significant parts of RSCo and GW style. In July 1960, TCB to Amersham (another Type 1 box – see *SB*, Plate 350) was instituted, and in March 1975, Supplementary AB was added, enabling Great Missenden to be switched out, as seen here. The box is 29 miles from Marylebone.

Plate 102
One of the Doncaster built Class 56s, No. 56065, approaches Worksop with a mgr train for one of the Trent Valley coal fired power stations on 27th May 1987. Following the government's decision to concentrate on coal extraction in its National Fuel Policy, BR placed an order with Brush Traction Limited in September 1974 for a new heavy duty freight locomotive. Half of the original batch of sixty, were built by BREL (Doncaster). The first was delivered on 29th April 1977. In the eventuality, Doncaster built 85 locomotives (Nos 56031 – 56115) over a six year period.

Many of the earliest boxes were square in plan, often about 13 feet, with the roof rising to the centre, on top of which there was frequently an ornamental finial. Unfortunately, Worksop West, the sole surviving MS&L Type 1 cabin, of 1874, has lost its large ball and spike finial (see *SB*, Plate 175), but the other elements of its very distinctive style can still be admired: 5in vertical battened boarding, and long thin operating floor windows. In the distance, Shireoaks East box (see Plate 34) can just be seen. No. 16 signal, behind the lamp post on the left, has a miniature arm and two-way stencil route indicator, showing R for the Down Reception line, and G for the Down Goods line.

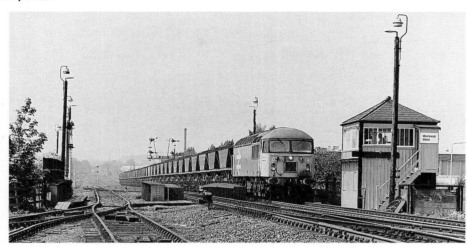

Plate 103
Class 47/0 No. 47297 heads a rake of ten empty (TOPS code) HEA hoppers past Rotherham Road with a trip to Doncaster Belmont on 30th May 1985. Passenger services along this line formerly originated from Sheffield Victoria. In October 1965, they were diverted onto the parallel ex-MR main line, leaving the former GC route handling freight traffic only. With the construction of the Holmes Curve, and the reopening of Rotherham Central, a passenger service was reintroduced to the line and the poorly located Masborough station was closed on 2nd October 1988.

The MS&L Type 2 established the genre of succeeding designs and in particular heralded the advent of gabled roofs as a permanent feature. Attractive bargeboards, finials, and a 2 panes by 2 opening gable vent, with similar operating floor windows were provided. But, at Rotherham Road, weatherboarding of the type 3 design, introduced circa 1888, combined to produce a hybrid, which was erected secondhand in 1909. During World War II, an independent brick wall surround was constructed in an attempt to afford some protection to the signalling apparatus from possible damage by enemy aircraft. Rotherham Road achieved fame in "The Times" of 17th July 1973, with a front page photograph of the signalman in his cabin, completely surrounded by flood water. There had been a record rainfall the previous day! The box retained its GC/RSCo 32 lever frame until closure on 12th April 1987, when the new Holmes Curve, controlled from Sheffield PSB was commissioned.

Plate 104
Having already serviced High Marnham Power Station with a working from Bevercotes Colliery, Class 58 No. 58032 propels its loaded (TOPS code) HAA hoppers past Ollerton Colliery cabin on 7th April 1988 prior to crossing over to the Up line and heading 7G34, the 12.32 Ollerton Colliery to High Marnham mgr service. (The rapid loader at the colliery can be seen to the right of the train.)

The final GC design, Type 5, first appeared in the late 1890s and lasted until about 1930. About 80 timber examples were built, and a copy of the original Westinghouse drawings for Ollerton Colliery appear in *SB*, Plate 181. The flat roof brick loo and concrete coal bunker are of course accretions. The cabin, erected in 1926 by the signalling contractor, accommodates a 30 lever, GC pattern frame and an IFS panel to control the former Boughton Junction signal box area and the single lines to Bevercotes, and High Marnham. The panel was commissioned in July 1984, after Boughton Junction box had been damaged beyond repair during the miners' strike.

Plate 105
On 15th August 1984, Class 47/0 No. 47237 eases the 06.25 Speedlink service from Warrington Arpley past Dee Marsh Junction, and prepares to enter Shotwick Sidings. This short train is composed of a loaded (TOPS code) BBA carrying steel coil and an international Deguna tank. Despite the reopening of the direct line to Mickle Trafford on 1st September 1986, 7D26 continues to make the longer journey to service Chester, Wrexham and Penyffordd. (The direct route had temporarily closed a couple of months before this photograph was taken.)

Opened in circa 1931, Dee Marsh Junction, illustrates the brick version of the GC Type 5 design, of which roughly 25 were built. Note the window detail of the platelayer's hut on the right – a contemporaneous facsimile of the cabin's locking room windows. The large opening vent in the wooden gable end above the nameboard is another typical feature of this design, which was itself very closely modelled on the MS&L brick Type 4. Since track rationalisation, the RSCo lever frame has been reduced in size to 25 levers.

Plate 106
Before gaining access to the Ketton Cement Terminal
on 17th April 1984, Class 31/1 No. 31109 propels the
9R12 trip over the trailing crossover at Wymondham
South Junction. It had earlier worked down the Dereham branch with the Polybulk wagons from the R.J.
Seaman & Sons grain terminal. After attaching cement
wagons, the train completed its journey to Norwich.

**Wymondham South, of 1877, is an early version of the
GE Type 2 design, which signalled a change to gabled
roofs. Large numbers were constructed of wood, with
horizontal weatherboarding and either notched or plain
(as here) bargeboards, but no finials were added. The
locking room windows, not seen on this rear view, followed the same vertical format as the operating floor
windows, which are unusual, being shallower than the
5 feet deep ones normally found on this design. The
nameboard and cabin steps are later replacements.
Wymondham South nestles in the vee formed by the
junction of the North Elmham single line (lower right-
hand foreground) with the Down Main, and works AB
to Spooner Row (to the right of the picture) and since
28th June 1987, TCB to Colchester PSB (see Plate 205).**

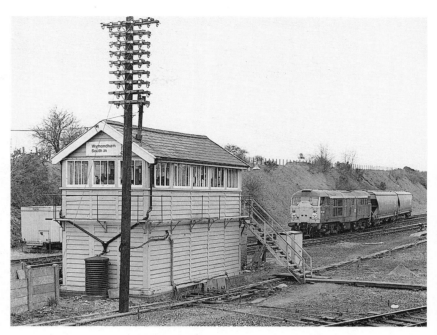

Plate 107
The stopping passenger service at Mellis was discontinued 18 years before this photograph was taken on 17th April 1984. One
year later, the masts for the 25kV overhead electrification to Norwich were placed in position, and the section was energised in
December 1986. The train is the 16.25 Norwich to Liverpool Street headed by Class 47/4 No. 47573. In a ceremony at Liverpool
Street station, on the day before the launch of Network SouthEast, the locomotive was named *The London Standard*. For the occasion, this Stratford based machine, became the first Class 47 to acquire the renamed sector livery.

**Dating from 1883, Mellis Junction was built a year after the GE began introducing brick as the main medium of box construction.
Of the less numerous Type 4/S&F design, it had a panelled brick base, with large attractive segmental-arched locking room windows,
complementing the then new 4-panes deep first floor windows, in sashes 3-panes across. Horizontal weatherboarding, plain bargeboards,
McK&H-type decorated fascia boards and a gently-pitched gabled roof completed the design. As its name implied, Mellis once controlled the junction of the Eye branch, which left the Up Main, on which the train was travelling, and went off behind the box to the
right. It was closed on 15th June 1986 when TCB working from Colchester PSB was extended to Diss.**

Plate 108
The 6.25kV ac electrification between Clapton Junction and Cheshunt Junction was completed in 1969 and converted to standard 25kV ac in 1983. Coming off the northerly end of this 8 mile 33 chain section, Class 315 emu set No. 315803 forms the 15.48 Liverpool Street to Hertford East local service on 22nd August 1987. The first Class 315 emus entered public service on Shenfield line trains at the end of 1980.

Situated 13 miles 71 chains from Liverpool Street station on the Up side at the London end of the station, Cheshunt Junction is a GE Type 8 box, built in 1891 by McK&H in connection with the opening of the new Cheshunt Loop line. Features associated with Type 4 are readily identifiable but here the operating floor windows are now in 3 by 3-pane sashes, the gabled roof, with ornamental ridge tiles, is more steeply pitched and a small vent in the gable end has been provided. Today, Cheshunt is equipped with a small 'N-X' panel working TCB to Brimsdown (see Plate 168), Broxbourne (Plate 204) and Enfield Town.

Plate 109
The end of the Sheringham branch is the only part of the BR passenger network in Norfolk that is not of GE origin. Beyond Roughton Road (a new station opened in 1985 to serve the southern side of Cromer), the last six miles of the branch follow the former Norfolk & Suffolk Joint and later, the ex-M&GN lines. Closure of the former GE terminus in September 1954 – renamed Cromer High in 1948 – and the concentration of services on the former M&GN Beach station benefited the residents and the bulk of visitors. This station was nearer to the centre of town and the beach. On 24th August 1988, Class 101 dmu (cars 54351 and 51177) forms the 16.50 Sheringham to Norwich service.

Although it is a non-standard design, Cromer has been included in this architectural survey for the sake of completeness because it is the only M&GN cabin to survive in use today. It is thought to date from circa 1914 and currently houses a 35 lever, RSCo frame, which controls the confluence of two single lines, one from London (left), worked by the EKT regulations to North Walsham box, and the other from Sheringham (right), worked on the OTW principle. Note the apparatus and signalman's platform for delivering and collecting the single line authorities to and from the drivers.

Plate 110

Working on the original Stockton & Darlington Railway route, a Class 101 2-car dmu (cars 54367 and 53165) draws out of Heighington with the 08.51 Saltburn to Bishop Auckland service on 7th February 1986. The train has just left the section from Charity Junction which was singled as part of the Darlington resignalling scheme in June 1972. (Implementation of the scheme was delayed a month by industrial trouble.) The signal boxes at Parkgate, Hopetown and Charity were amongst the casualties of the changes.

Until 1899, the NE was divided into three Divisions: Northern, Central and Southern, each with independent responsibility for engineering. Each designed their own cabins and employed different building and signalling contractors. Dating from circa 1872, Heighington is a Central Division Type C1a, which possibly originated from a Stockton & Darlington design of the 1860s. All these cabins were gabled, of brick to roof construction, with the size of the operating floor reduced by the stepped brickwork. Two distinctive locking room windows at the front of the end elevations, magnificent bargeboards with intersecting cross-timbers, and finials over six feet long (unfortunately removed many years ago), and tall chimneys completed the design. Note the cast iron DP plate on the box front: this meant Distance Point, and was placed at the average centre of the platforms of a through station. The re-miling of the NE and numbering of bridges was carried out in 1905.

Plate 111

Few trains are scheduled along the Leamside line and even less actually use it! After 11th August 1986 the signal boxes were no longer continuously manned and services such as 6O44, the 16.06 Tyneside Central Freight Depot (TCFD) to Paddock Wood Speedlink were re-routed via the ECML. On the ultimate week before diversion, Class 47/0 No. 47231 heads the train past Usworth on 4th August 1986. Now designated 6L98, this train terminates at Ripple Lane and since the closure of Tyne Yard, has started at Doncaster Belmont. Today, traffic from TCFD is carried on 6N74, the 12, 13 Hexham–Tees Yard Speedlink service.

Where space was at a premium – it seemed to be more so on the Northern Division – the NE built either bridge (Type N5) or cantilever cabins. Usworth is an example of the latter, erected in 1898, to Type N2c (c = cantilever). This design retained the main features of Type N1: brick construction, hipped roof and porch; but it incorporated triple locking room windows with individual stone sills, mullions and lintels. Here, the windows were bricked up in 1982, when an IFS panel replaced the 21 lever, McK&H, No. 17 pattern frame, of 1947. The gates and therefore the gate wheel had been replaced by MCB and a pedestal push button control unit in September 1977. Go and see Usworth before it is closed in 1991 under the ECML electrification scheme.

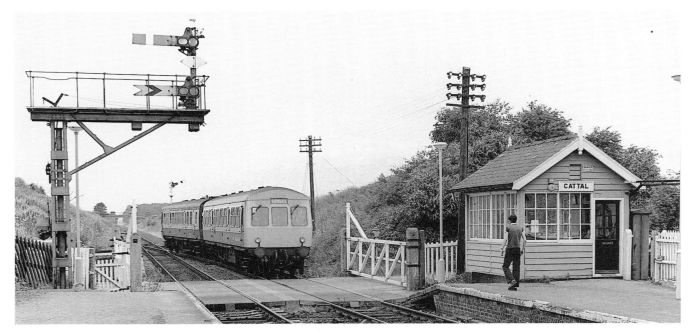

Plate 112
The afternoon peace of 14th July 1984 is briefly interrupted as the 13.30 Leeds to York (via Harrogate) service enters Cattal, formed from a Class 101 2-car dmu (cars 51504 and 51430).

With the increase of road traffic and the expansion of the system from about 1900, the NE Southern Division increasingly used timber for small and/or ground level boxes at level crossings and country stations, often as a later alternative to the Type S1b. Here is Cattal, a Type S5, with weatherboarding, three-panes deep windows, and finials. The nameboard is the wooden LNER design; NE enamel name signs were invariably placed immediately below the front windows in the centre. They were 8in deep, with a 1½in cream border, and 3in cream letters, in a chocolate surround. The gates are worked by key locks from lever 15, (see Plate 136), and the signalman is about to collect the single line key token for the section from Knaresborough (the line was singled using the former Down Main in 1972). Note the position of the diamond sign – it refers to No. 11 Down Main Starter and not to Whixley Gates Crossing distant signal below.

Plate 113
Trains between Manchester and Chester via Northwich formerly ran between the ex-CLC stations at Manchester Central and Chester Northgate. It was not until 5th May 1969, after a new junction at Cornbrook had been commissioned the previous weekend, that services were diverted to use Oxford Road. Later the same year, on 7th September 1969, the opening of a new curve at Mickle Trafford allowed trains to be re-routed into Chester General. Leaving Mobberley on 8th August 1987, is the 14.00 Oxford Road to Chester service composed of a Class 108 two-car set dmu (cars 51902 and 54485).

Most of the early CLC Type 1 cabins were built of timber, with stout corner posts, vertical boarding, porches and 2 by 2-panes locking room windows. The upper floor windows were 3 by 3-panes, with sliding sashes by the front corner posts only. The wooden nameboard was placed in the front centre, below the upper windows. Dating from 1886, Mobberley is the sole surviving Type 1b box. This type's refinements concerned the roof details: a more prominent roof overhang and large eaves brackets. All Type 1 roofs were hipped. Mobberley retains its original CLC 16 lever frame and controls the level crossing by MCB.

Plate 114
On 2nd June 1988 Old Oak Common based Class 47/4 No. 47484 *Isambard Kingdom Brunel* makes a glorious sight as it approaches Montrose with a track recording special bound for Aberdeen. The train has just crossed the viaduct over the Inner Basin, designed by Thomas Bouch, the engineer responsible for the first Tay Bridge. The locomotive was repainted in January 1985 to celebrate the 150th anniversary of the GWR. It first emerged from

Crewe Works in a shade of green that offended many enthusiasts. To atone, a revised livery was applied, and in true GW tradition, brass number and nameplates were used. Three other Class 47s were similarly treated: Class 47/0 No. 47079 *G.J. Churchward* and Class 47/4s Nos 47500 *Great Western* and 47628 *Sir Daniel Gooch.*

NB Type 1 boxes, dating from the period 1878 to 1884, were very plentiful on the Arbroath to Kinnaber Junction, and Edinburgh Suburban lines. Montrose South, with her surviving sisters at Montrose North and Inverkeilor, were opened in 1881. All were constructed of brick, with hipped roofs, brick chimneys and porches. The locking room windows had segmental arches, and the operating floor windows, here very much altered, were originally 2 by 2-panes, above which there was panelled woodwork with diagonal boarding. The cabin houses a 42 lever, Stevens frame, of circa 1914, and works AB to the North box (on the main lines), and TB on the two mile single line south to Usan. A new style road type retro-reflective PSR sign (50 mph) applies over the double to single line points.

Plate 115
When the Buchanan Street terminus closed on 7th November 1966 all services, with the exception of those to/from Cumbernauld, were diverted to Queen Street and, for over 20 years, through passengers had to change at Springburn. An example of the connecting service – the 08.20 Milngavie to Springburn – passes High Street Junction on 14th April 1987, composed of Class 303 emu No. 303069. A direct service between Cumbernauld and Queen Street, with a reversal at Cowlairs, was initiated in May 1989.

High Street East Junction cannot be categorised. The only feature present in this design, reminiscent of NB practice is the Type 4 locking room windows. Extended in similar style around 1908 to house a 150 lever frame, the box contained an 'N-X' panel, commissioned in 1982, and worked AB to Bellgrove cabin (to the left) and TCB to Hyndland. Much track abandonment was also carried out in 1982: the Old Barracks Coal Depot (to the left of the signal box) and the lines around High Street Goods box (beyond the bridge on the extreme right), closed on 5th November 1967 when Yard Working was introduced, have all been lifted. Under postponed Stage 4 of the Glasgow North resignalling scheme, High Street together with Hyndland closed on 19th November 1989.

Plate 116
The survival of the West Highland line during the "Beeching" years was in part due to the proposed wood pulp mill near Annat. On 16th August 1984, Class 37/0 No. 37039 arrives at Mallaig Junction with 7B05, the 13.30 Mossend to Corpach Speedlink service. The train was propelled behind the cabin before the locomotive ran round to make the short journey to the paper mill. Today all West Highland freight traffic works via Mossend. Before this, all activity was centred on Sighthill, while prior to December 1980, Cadder was the originating yard.

The West Highland line boxes of 1894 were of two styles. Mallaig Junction is a NB Type 6b, with round-arched locking room windows and sub-divided panes in the top of the operating floor windows. Despite its name (it was the junction for Mallaig), the box is in fact only $\frac{3}{4}$ mile from Fort William station, and has recently been renamed Fort William Junction, to avoid possible confusion with Mallaig station, when RETB was inaugurated from Banavie Signalling Centre on 6th December 1987. Note the (now redundant) token exchange platforms for the Banavie (left) and Spean Bridge (right) single line sections, and the running subsidiary shunt signal, No. 26, to the left of the locomotive, provided for shunting movements into the Loop and Storage Sidings behind the box. This had to be cleared before the main running signals for a train to Spean Bridge were pulled off.

Plate 117
Elgin East Goods Yard is all that remains of the GNoS network that formerly radiated from Elgin. Standing in the yard, is the 6H12 trip on 3rd June 1988 composed of five Polybulk wagons. Having run round its train, Class 47/0 No. 47210 waits for the 13.30 Inverness to Aberdeen passenger service to clear the single line section from Forres, before departing for the Scottish Malt Distillers works at Burghead via Alves Junction.

Introduced about 1884 and lasting until about 1900, the GNoS Type 2 design accounted for over half of that company's signal boxes. The majority of the cabins were gabled, of timber construction, with porches and small horizontal locking room windows. Below these, hinged hatches were provided to facilitate access to the equipment for the maintenance staff. Opened as Elgin West on 1st May 1884, and renamed Elgin Centre in 1934, this box contained a 50 lever frame until closure on 11th November 1973, when it was converted for use as staff accommodation. Now the steps to the porch have been removed and only Insch and Huntly South survive as Type 2 cabins in signalling use.

Plate 118
Departing from East Farleigh, on the "Medway Valley" line, Class 415/1 (4-EPB) emu No. 5031 forms the 11.08 Strood to Paddock Wood train on 23rd August 1983. As part of a face-lifting programme, this unit has since had the compartments converted into open saloons and is now a Class 415/4 (4-EPB) and renumbered No. 5484. Today, the normal service on the line is covered by Class 411 (4-CEP) sets.

East Farleigh is a rare example of the juxtaposition of the same design for both signal box and station buildings. In fact, this style had originated with the formation of the SE in 1842, and was widely used for minor stations. Typical features are the vertical sash windows, weatherboarding, and hipped roof with lead flashings. Dating from 1892, East Farleigh contains a SE 5in pitch, 25 lever, tappet locking frame, 17 of which are now spare. It works AB to Wateringbury and Maidstone West. The two gates are released by key locks from No. 7 lever, (see Plate 136) and No. 23 Up Main Starter, seen in the off position, is only seven yards from the level crossing.

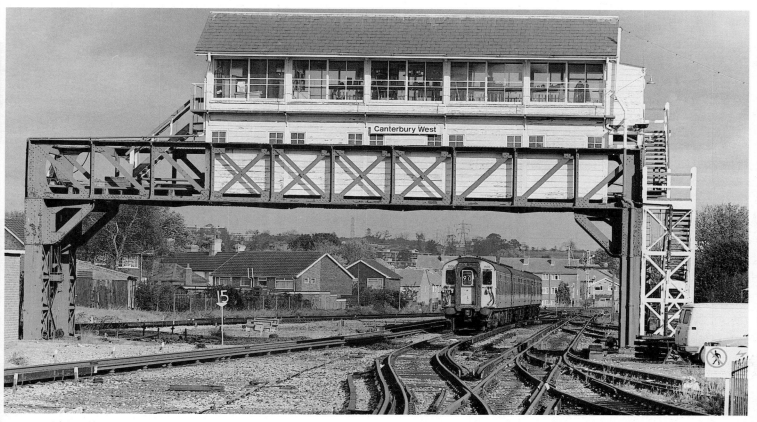

Plate 119
Approaching Canterbury West on 27th October 1988, Class 411/4 (refurbished 4-CEP) 4-car emu No. 1502 forms the 11.07 Margate to Charing Cross service. Upgrading of these units was designed to increase their life by approximately 15 years. Changes included the conversion of the second class accommodation to open saloons and the fitting of fluorescent lighting. (This set, formerly No. 7104, was one of the initial batch.) It went to Swindon for refurbishment in August 1980 and was returned to the Southern Region the following December carrying the number 411502. It was one of the last sets to be allocated a six digit number and was shortly afterwards truncated to its present designation.

Built in 1905, Canterbury West is an imposing SE example of a bridge box on a steel gantry. The cabin structure itself is to the S&F Type 12b design. Type 12 cabins were built either of brick (see Plate 124) or timber, and obviously to reduce the weight on the gantry, timber was chosen. Small, square 2 by 2-panes locking room windows, and operating floor windows (also 2 by 2), with horizontal lapped boarding and a gabled roof gave this design a somewhat plain appearance. On a girder for 96 levers, the Sykes & Hallam patent design, $4\frac{1}{2}$in centres, tappet locking frame is at right angles to the track, with the signalman facing the photographer when operating the levers. The closure of the Whitstable Harbour and Bishopsbourne lines, together with the lifting of the two through lines has resulted in only 46 of the remaining 72 levers being in use.

Plate 120
The 12.16 Portsmouth Harbour to Waterloo train leaves Petersfield on 27th August 1983. The service is made up of two Class 423 (4-VEP) emus – with No. 7822 (since renumbered No. 3122) trailing. The trackbed to the right was part of the Midhurst branch which closed to all traffic in 1955. This 21 mile branch formerly continued to Pulborough and connected the two main routes from London to Portsmouth.

Unique now in two respects, Petersfield is the only one of three surviving LSW Type 3a examples to remain in use as an operational signal box and to have had this style of ornamental valancing fitted – standard on Type 2 cabins, from which this design is derived. Built probably circa 1884, it incorporates a panelled brick ground floor, with segmental arched locking room windows (now bricked up), and a wooden superstructure, with operating floor windows four panes deep in sashes three panes across, and a hipped roof. A walkway for cleaning the windows was not provided. Extended at the London (far) end, Petersfield is situated on the Up side, at 54 miles 71 chains from Waterloo. It now houses only a ten lever Stevens frame and an IFS panel, working TCB to Haslemere and Havant.

Plate 121
Class 33/0 No. 33004 approaches Clapham Junction with the 16.38(FX) London Waterloo to Salisbury train on 27th August 1981. (On Fridays, this service was extended to Yeovil Junction.) In 1971, Class 33s displaced 'Warship' Class 42/43s on the ex-LSW West of England Main Line, and in turn, in May 1981, had given way to Class 50s, which were surplus to BR(WR) requirements due to increased use of HSTs on the ex-GW routes out of Paddington. The 33s continued to find regular use on the Salisbury stopping trains until May 1989.

Over the years, there have been several bridge cabins on the LSW main line between Waterloo and Clapham Junction, but only West London Junction and Clapham "A" survive today. The latter has had a chequered career. Opened in 1905, it defies architectural classification, consisting merely of a series of interconnecting sheds on a bowstring-girder bridge. During World War II, a steel roof weighing about 40 tons, was added as an air-raid precaution. The framework for this is clearly visible. It was removed in 1965, after the bridge subsided some $3\frac{1}{2}$ feet at the London side, northern (left-hand) corner, on Monday 10th May, at about 08.40, resulting in the complete suspension of the Waterloo train service. The subsidence was caused by the fracture of two tensioned lattice supports between the upper and lower members of a bowstring girder. The cause of the fracture was rust. Under Stage 7b of the Waterloo Area Resignalling Scheme (WARS to its friends), Clapham "A" closed in May 1990, the area now being controlled from a PSB at Wimbledon.

Plate 122
On 24th August 1983, Class 423 (4-VEP) No. 7863 emu (since renumbered No. 3163) prepares to halt the 08.55 Victoria to Dover Priory stopping service at Shepherd's Well. To the left is a rake of loaded (TOPS code) MDV 21 tonne mineral wagons that had earlier come from Tilman-stone Colliery. Traffic over this branch (diverging to the right) ceased in 1984 and never resumed after the year long National Union of Mineworkers' strike.

Yet another sole survivor, Shepherd's Well, circa 1878, is a standard LCD gabled design, with vertical board-ing and three-panes deep operating floor windows, in sliding sashes. A single locking room window (2 by 2-panes) in the front centre of the brick base, a porch, and vents above the nameboard are provided. Two finials complete the design. Shepherd's Well still retains its original LCD pattern, 23 lever frame, and works AB to Canterbury East and TCB to Dover Priory signal boxes.

Plate 123
Oxted joined the Southern Region's 'third rail' network when the East Grinstead line was energised on 5th October 1987. Prior to the change, a Class 207 demu No. 1313 (since renumbered No. 207013) forms an Up ECS working on the evening of 22nd August 1983. With the exception of a few peak period services, these sets now only work on the Uckfield to Oxted section.

There were three versions of the LBSC Type 2 design, which was built from 1880 onwards. The timber variety had horizontal lapped boarding, almost square 2 panes by 2 locking room windows, and upper floor windows two panes deep, the sliding sashes two or three panes across. All had hipped roofs. With a S&F ventilator, Oxted was one of the last Type 2c cabins to be built. Opened in 1896, with a 29 lever, LBSC frame, it was closed on 11th July 1987, leaving Seaford as the only Type 2c survivor. The attractive bracket signal, complete with finial, seen here, was removed with the commissioning of the new brick-built Oxted box, (off the left of the picture), containing the BR(SR)'s first SSI panel.

Plate 124
Class 411 (4-CEP) emu No. 1551 passes through Sturry with the 13.12 Margate to Charing Cross train on 24th August 1983. A decision in 1985 resulted in this set acquiring the so-called "Jaffa Cake" livery. This policy has since been reversed in favour of the application of the more widespread "Network SouthEast" colours for the 'Kent Coast' electrics.

The S&F Type 12a design first appeared around 1884 and many of the BTF versions were built on the SE. These examples had a pronounced overhang to the roof at the front and back, and 2-panes deep upper floor windows in sliding sashes, with a segmental-arched locking room window. Here at Sturry, the arch is formed of two courses of headers, and the cabin sits neatly on its plinth, topped by a course of splayed bricks known as plinth stretchers. The roof tiles, guttering and drain-pipes are recent replacements. Sturry has been a gate box for over 20 years, and contains a 19 lever, 4in centres, S&F frame on a beam for 22 levers.

Plate 125
But for the intervention of the Minister of Transport, BR would have withdrawn all remaining services on the Isle of Wight in the mid-1960s. Closure of the Ryde to Shanklin section was rejected because of the hardship that would have been caused to the many summer tourists who use the line. The full electrified service, which opened on 20th March 1967, resulted from the minister's edict that money must be spent on the section left open. Tight clearances precluded the transfer of conventional stock, and as a result services have been worked by redundant LT tube stock. The first example, driving trailer S38S of 3-TIS unit No. 037, arrived on 1st September 1965. Its first outing, for gauging tests, was on 4th September, when it was hauled by Class O2 0-4-4T No. 24 *Calbourne*. An example of this antiquated stock, Class 485 No. 485042, is seen entering Sandown station with the 13.07 Shanklin to Ryde Pier service on 28th August 1988. Two months later, Sandown was reduced to a passing loop when the section between Sandown and Brading was singled in connection with resignalling work.

In 1988, Sandown was one of only three cabins still in use on the Isle of Wight, and the sole S&F timber Type 12b to survive in its original location. Built in 1893, on the Up platform, it was a tall box, providing the signalman with a view over the since-demolished station canopy. Access to the operating floor was via an internal staircase from the platform. It was equipped with a S&F duplex 1888 patent, 4in centres, 32 lever frame. Extensive resignalling was carried out in connection with the electrification of the Isle of Wight system in 1967, since when Ryde Pier Head and Shanklin cabins have been closed. With Brading, Sandown closed officially on 30th October 1988, when a panel in Ryde St Johns Road box assumed control of the entire island system.

7 : Level Crossing Protection

Plate 126
The BRC&W 'Calder Valley' sets entered public service on the ex-L&Y main line via Todmorden on 1st January 1962. Destinations included long gone termini such as Liverpool Exchange, Leeds Central and Bradford Exchange (rebuilt and renamed Bradford Interchange). Nowadays, better known as Class 110 dmus, many of the surviving sets – like that illustrated – have lost their centre cars. The view shows the 09.47 Sheffield to Cleethorpes train (composed of cars 51823 and 51843) approaching a rather disconsolate pedestrian at Great Coates on 2nd September 1987.

The 1839 and 1845 Acts of Parliament required that all railways should be fenced and that where a line crossed a public road on the level, heavy wooden gates, which could be swung alternately across the road and railway, should be provided. Hand-operated by an attendant or remotely from an adjacent signal box by means of a 'ship's wheel' connected to rodding, the gates – for more than a century, the traditional form of public level crossing protection – are normally closed across the railway and swung through 90° when a train is approaching. When the gates are closed across the road, the mechanical interlocking in the lever frame permits the signals protecting the crossing to be cleared. Conversely, the gates cannot be opened to road traffic while any protecting railway signal displays 'proceed' to railway traffic. At the end of 1989, there were roughly 440 manned gated crossings, interlocked with railway signals. Great Coates was a MS&L Type 2 box of 1884 and was closed on 18th October 1987 when AHB (see Plate 133), supervised from Marsh Junction, were introduced.

Plate 127
After traversing the picturesque Esk Valley line, the 12.16 Whitby to Darlington service passes North Ormesby on 24th April 1987 and slows down to meet the main line at Guisborough Junction (0 mile 38 chains distant). The Class 143 'Pacer' No. 143002, which formed this service, was disbanded late in 1987, and car No. 55643 was attached to 55676 to form a temporary formation No. 143026 (later renumbered No. 143010 in the middle of 1988).

At North Ormesby, a new line in crossing gates was installed in the early 1960s. Known as boom gates, they give the appearance of a low garden fence, are constructed of wood throughout and are painted red and white. They have solid rubber-tyred wheels for smooth operation, and are powered by small electric motors, mounted below the booms. The recently demolished footbridge was built parallel with the road, after the box and partly through its hipped roof. The cabin itself was a NE Type C1 and was down-graded to a gate-box on 26th January 1986, when the line was singled between Guisborough Junction (worked from Middlesbrough PSB) and Nunthorpe.

Plate 128

A scheme to eliminate the main level crossings at Lincoln was passed in 1938, but was abandoned because of World War II. It was not until 1955 that the Minister of Transport & Civil Aviation approved plans to construct a viaduct at Pelham Street, the southernmost of these crossings. However, High Street and Brayford level crossings remain in use over fifty years after the original plans were drawn up. Located between High Street and Pelham Street, Lincoln Central is seen with Class 150/1 'Sprinter' No. 150107, at platform 6, forming the 13.35 service for Birmingham New Street on 23rd May 1987. Prior to the opening of the Boultham curve on 13th May 1985, these trains operated from the now closed St Marks station.

The level crossing gates at High Street, were so large and heavy that they were converted to power operation in September 1925. A matching extension to the cabin (a GN Type 1) was built to house a two miniature lever frame (in the upper storey), which controls an electric motor (on the ground floor), to which is attached the rodding to work the gates mechanically. During peak periods, the signalman often had difficulty in finding breaks in the road traffic, so traffic lights were introduced at this level crossing as early as 1956. The operation of the miniature levers simultaneously actuates the traffic signals and the newer audible warning devices. One of these "Yodalarm" units can be seen fixed to the wood post in the right-hand corner of the crossing, above the lady's head. Lincoln is another preserve of semaphore signalling – but for how long?

Plate 129

Almost thirty years after the arrival of the first dmu on Tyneside in September 1955, the first Class 143 set was delivered to Heaton on 7th August 1985. A year later on 20th August 1986 'Pacer' No. 143012 forming the 08.43(SX) Carlisle to Middlesbrough service passes through East Boldon. In the distance is Tile Shed signal box which was remote from, and at right angles to, the Durham Coast line. Located in the fork between the Newcastle line and the former route to South Shields, it was closed in December 1988.

In the BTC Act of 1954, lifting barriers in lieu of swinging gates, were permitted to be installed. So the former BR(NER) was quick off the mark in the design and manufacture of mechanical lifting barriers, which have twin timber booms, pivoted on roller bearings and are fitted with light alloy "skirts". To control the balance at all angles, sliding weights are used, which reduce the physical effort required to raise or lower the booms. The signalman operates the barriers by a single gate purchase wheel. The drive is by rack and pinion, the latter rotating a slotted arm through 270°, while the barrier reaches maximum speed at $42\frac{1}{2}°$, halfway through the sequence. Of a total of about 20 BR(NER) crossings so equipped over a twenty year period, six other examples at Norton-on-Tees, Nunthorpe, Barton Hill, Driffield, Cave Crossing and Rigton still exist.

Plate 130
Nearing the end of its short revenue-earning life, Class 210 Derby built 3-car demu No. 210002 passes Colthrop Siding with the 18.07 Bedwyn to Reading local service on 21st August 1987. When constructed in 1981, this prototype was seen as a possible stop gap pending electrification. It was envisaged that members of the class would be compatible with emus (externally similar to Class 455 emus) and be detached for running on non-electrified sections. They turned out to be very much more expensive to construct when compared with the various 'Sprinter' types that have subsequently gained favour with the Provincial Sector. It was withdrawn by the Western Region in January 1988.

Power-worked MCB began to be introduced on a grand scale nationwide in the middle 1960s. The crossings are provided with audible warning devices, traffic lights (steady amber for five seconds, followed by twin flashing reds) and barriers with boom skirts, which, when lowered, completely fence off the railway from the road user. Besides supervising its own crossing situated between two paper mills, Colthrop Siding box also controls Midgham station and Thatcham station crossings by CCTV. Each of the three crossings is protected by a colour light signal, operated to clear by the signalman, after the barriers have been proved locked in the lowered position and he has pressed the "crossing clear" button. A comprehensive article on Colthrop Crossing appeared in the "Railway Magazine" for March 1984.

Plate 131
The MCB crossing at Dunham Massey was equipped with two pairs of skirted half-barriers as an alternative to the full-length barriers at Colthrop. Telephones for road users are not now provided at MCBs. At the end of 1989, there were just over 320 MCB on BR – a reduction of about 80 since the end of 1977 – almost all having been converted to CCTV operation (see Plate 185). Dunham Massey box, a S&F Type 6 of 1872, on the LNW, closed on 7th July 1985 with the line from Skelton Junction (Altrincham) to Arpley Junction (Warrington) and was relatively intact when this photograph was taken on 8th August 1987.

Plate 132
In the early 1960s there was talk of axing the ECML north of Newcastle. It was argued that the planned electrification of the WCML could only be justified if all Anglo-Scottish trunk traffic was concentrated on a single route! By 1991, however, a second electrified line will cross the border. In the last year before the catenary was erected, the 14.10 (SO) Edinburgh to King's Cross HST is seen passing Little Mill on 28th May 1988. At the time, Saturday services were given 20 minutes' recovery time to facilitate electrification work.

The early 1970s heralded the advent of CCTV as a means for the remote operation of former MCB crossings. Little Mill is just such an example: in August 1967, its traditional gates were replaced by MCB, which were in turn converted on 16th April 1978 to CCTV working, with surveillance and control from Alnmouth panel box, some 4½ miles away. The remote operator must obtain a view of the crossing on his monitor screen before the barrier equipment will function. When the barriers have descended, the signalman must press a "crossing clear" button before the protecting railway signals can be cleared. Automatic raising of the barriers after the passage of the train speeds up the operating cycle somewhat, but the major delay to road users is still during the approach of the train. The base of the 1870s' stone cabin, and the 1960s' brick relay room extension remains (left), while the lighting columns and twin camera mast support (right) frame the crossing. There were some 250 CCTV crossings in use at the end of 1989.

Plate 133
Even the nearby RAF base was not sufficient to prevent Kinloss station from closing. Since 1937, the number of intermediate stations on the Aberdeen–Inverness route has been reduced from 32 to just eight. The majority, including Kinloss, succumbed in the mid-1960s. Between December 1964 and May 1968, 23 closed and only one, Dyce, has subsequently reopened. Approaching the disused station, Class 47/4 No. 47641 *Fife Region* heads the 10.38 Inverness to Aberdeen train on 27th July 1988.

Section 66 of the BTC Act of 1957 gave the Minister of Transport powers to authorise "such barriers ... and automatic and other devices" for the modernisation of crossings. Thus at AHB crossings, the approach of a train activates road traffic signals, audible warnings (for pedestrians) and the lowering of a barrier on each side of the railway, across the left hand side only of the road. The warning sequence is similar to MCB: after 4 to 8 seconds of flashing red lights, the barriers begin to descend and are fully lowered 6 to 8 seconds later. The fastest train is timed to arrive not less than 27 seconds after the amber lights first show. AHB are not interlocked with the rail signals and are permitted only on single and double track lines where the maximum train speed is 100 mph. On single lines, at Kinloss (West), for example, the "Another Train Coming" signs are not needed. Note the cattle-cum-trespass guard rails in the foreground, now a mandatory feature at almost all modernised crossings.

Plate 134
On 15th July 1984, Class 47/0 No. 47033 is working hard lifting the 1Z38 Wellingborough to Whitby excursion from the Tees lowlands towards the North Yorkshire Moors. It is passing through the then recently opened Gypsy Lane station that serves an affluent suburban development on the southern fringe of Middlesbrough. Today, all traffic uses the former Up platform at this station.

The BR(NER) was at the forefront of the development of automatic open level crossings for use at lightly trafficked rural locations. The prototype at Yafforth (on the Wensleydale branch) was commissioned on Tuesday 10th September 1963, and has evolved into today's AOCL. Marton Lane AOCL was commissioned on 28th April 1983. As its name suggests, this type of crossing has no barriers
but protection for the road user is otherwise similar to an AHB. Telephones are not provided, but signs (left) give the number of the supervising railway office in the event of an emergency. The safe operation of the crossing is monitored locally by the driver, who at a point from which the crossing is visible and which is more than a safe stopping distance away, sees a flashing white light if his train has triggered the track side treadles. The driver's white light (on the post on the extreme right above the Gypsy Lane station nameplate) does not flash if the road traffic lights have failed or a main power supply failure has occurred. In these circumstances, the driver is instructed to stop short of the crossing and proceed over it with caution, and to report the fault as soon as possible (in the case of this Down train, at Nunthorpe signal box).

Plate 135
On 2nd August 1987, Class 37/0 No. 37131 heads a short ballast train onto the Down Loop at Porthmadog to allow the 10.15 (SuO) Pwllheli to Machynlleth service to pass. After the departure of the 'Sprinter', the two wagons which had been loaded near Penrhyn-deudraeth earlier that morning, were discharged to the east of the station, adjacent to the Welsh Highland Railway (left middle distance).

A white square with a black cross (known as a St George's Cross Advance Warning Board) is the first intimation a driver receives on the approach to an AOCL. Typically, it is placed some 300 to 600 yards, depending on the line speed and sighting conditions, before reaching a combined St Andrew's Cross/Speed Restriction sign, sited some 100 to 300 yards before the crossing. At Porthmadog, a MCB crossing, the St George's Cross for Traethmawr AOCL, 490 yards distant, is attached for convenience to the post of No. 2 Up Main Starter. A Dutton Type 2 design of about 1894, Porthmadog, originally the East box, was extended in 1932, when the West box was closed, to house a 38 lever, GW frame. It closed in October 1988 with the advent of RETB supervised from Machynlleth box.

Plate 136
The silhouette of Ferrybridge Power Station epitomises Railfreight's primary operations in the South Yorkshire area. On 3rd September 1987, Class 56 No. 56027 comes off the Up Goods Loop at England Lane with a mgr working for Drax Power Station. This locomotive was one of the original batch built by Craiova Works of Electroputere, Romania. The first arrived in England via Harwich in 1976, but it was the middle of 1980 before Healey Mills based examples largely displaced Class 47 locomotives on workings serving the Aire Valley power stations.

Modernisation has not yet reached England Lane – a manned gated crossing interlocked with railway signals. Protection is achieved by the gateman locking the gates across the road with two key locks, each like a small metal capital letter L, which are then inserted into a receptacle on lever No. 2 of the ground frame in the hut. Lever 2 is then placed in the normal position, mechanically locking the key locks in the ground frame, and the release lever (No. 1) is placed normal, thus locking No. 2 lever normal, and enabling the signalman at Knottingley panel box (the supervising block post), to turn his No. 644 release switch to normal. This electrically locks England Lane's No. 1 lever normal and frees the signal switches protecting the crossing.

Plate 137

Class 20s Nos 20306 and 20305 head 6N53, the 07.00 Tees Yard to Redmire service on 24th October 1986. The return working to the Redcar Mineral Terminal carries limestone for the British Steel Lackenby complex. Prior to their transfer to Thornaby, these slow-speed control locomotives had been working stone trains in the Buxton area. Shortly after this photograph was taken, the locomotives regained their former numbers Nos 20173 and 20172 and were distinguished by being named *Wensleydale* and *Redmire*. The use of these locomotives along the route was relatively short-lived and today, Class 37/5s are the usual motive power.

Wensley, situated 19 miles 65 chains from Castle Hills junction, Northallerton, became a TMO crossing nearly twenty years ago, using the existing boom gates, which have seen better days! Their motors were disconnected and removed and the gates became hand-worked and secured by padlock and chain against the railway. The keys, now kept at Low Gates box, are collected by the travelling line supervisor, who accompanies the train and works the numerous TMO crossings on the branch. The OTW block regulations for single lines are in operation from Castle Hills junction to Redmire, and the maximum permissible speed is 40 mph. St George's Cross Advance Warning boards and Stop boards protect the crossing in both directions.

Plate 138

The 6M90 Whitemoor to Cavendish Sidings Speedlink service delivered little traffic to Birkenhead on 28th August 1987. After depositing a couple of vans at the Stanton Grove Sidings (Vittoria Dock), Class 03 No. 03162 crosses Duke Street with one (TOPS code) HEA hopper for the coal depot at Birkenhead North. The shunter had been transferred from Gateshead to Merseyside in the summer of 1983 and repainted in green livery with original number (D2162) at the beginning of 1987. An inscription on the cabside commemorated the former Birkenhead Mollington Street steam/diesel depot which closed in November 1985.

Open Crossings (OC) are the simplest and cheapest form of protection permitted on public roads, (again authorised by Section 66 of the 1957 BTC Act). They are suitable where the train speed does not exceed 10 mph, and the train crew can see the crossing in normal visibility from a point 20 seconds distant at the crossing speed. Rail signs warn the crew of their approach to the crossing and their duty to stop or reduce speed before continuing over the road. Where the traffic level is less than 300 vehicles a day, the maximum speed of vehicles is 30 mph and there is clear visibility of trains, OC with no lights may be used. At Duke Street level crossing, however, traffic lights are installed and operated by the train crew.

Plate 139
On 2nd April 1986, evening commuters bide their time as Class 47/3 No. 47380 crosses Regent Road level crossing (in the north Liverpool dockland) with 4F67, the 17.40 Seaforth Container Terminal to Garston Freightliner Terminal. The latter was the site of the first container terminal on Merseyside, while Seaforth did not open until early 1980. The Alexandra Dock depot (to the right) was still being used by the Post Office, but closed a few weeks later when the traffic was transferred to the Spekeland Road Goods Depot at Edge Hill.

Regent Road crossing is a similar OC, but additionally is equipped with Miniature Red/Green Warning Lights (MWL) on the post on the extreme right, for the benefit of pedestrians. These train-controlled miniature traffic lights are displayed in instruction notice boards on each side of the crossing, and read: Red – Stop; Green – Clear; No Light – Beware. Often MWL, with either hand-operated gates or lifting barriers, and a telephone linking the crossing with a signal box, are installed on minor roads, an early example being Bardon Mill, in June 1966. Neither system monitoring equipment nor audible warning devices are provided. Because these crossings are subject to indiscipline by the road user, future MWL are to be restricted to private crossings.

8 : Survivors

Plate 140
Class 37/0 No. 37085 (since renumbered No. 37711 and named *Tremorfa Steel Works*) restarts the 14.05 Fort William to Mallaig service out of Banavie on 16th August 1984. At the conclusion of the previous summer's timetable, through workings between Glasgow Queen Street and Mallaig were discontinued but recommenced following the introduction of 'Super Sprinters'.

Signalling on the West Highland line has changed almost beyond recognition in the last few years. On 7th June 1987, Banavie cabin was reduced in status to a combined gate and bridge box (to control the southern end of the Caledonian Canal) in the Mallaig Junction – Annat EKT block section. A week later, it was closed and a new gate/bridge box commissioned. This became the West Highland line RETB control centre on 6th December 1987. The blockposts at Glenfinnan and Arisaig were closed, and Annat became a gate box. Four new RETB sections were inaugurated: Mallaig Junction–Loch Eil Outward Bound–Glenfinnan–Arisaig–Mallaig station. This lovely lattice signal complete with wire guys and finial was formerly Banavie's No. 9 Up Starter.

Plate 141
When first delivered, Class 40 No. 40060 was, in common with all the earlier examples, fitted with gangway doors and discs, but in 1965 all the Haymarket allocation (Nos D260-D266) had their front-ends modified and replaced by a centrally-mounted indicator panel. It is seen at Waverley station in May 1980 with an early evening parcels service. This locomotive was the first to be allocated to Haymarket (in February 1960) and it was the last to be withdrawn (on 23rd January 1985). However, it was subsequently resurrected twice! Between February 4th and 8th, it was used to pilot electrically hauled trains out of Kingmoor Yard while repairs were carried out to the catenary. Later, on 27th April 1985, it was reinstated as Departmental locomotive No. 97405 to work on the remodelling at Crewe. It was not withdrawn until 4th March 1987, outliving all other Departmental Class 40s, and was finally cut up at Vic Berry's early in 1988.

Since its opening in 1893, Edinburgh Waverley station has been resignalled twice, the last time in 1976, when a simplified track layout and modern colour lights were installed. The cabin in the centre background however is a relic of the original signalling supplied by the RSCo of Fazakerley, Liverpool. It was the smallest of the four boxes, contained a 34 lever frame and was formerly known as North box, which, with its sister, South, worked scissor crossovers and a few other connections in the centre of the long through platforms. Its working life as a cabin ceased on 11th October 1936 when a new 227 lever power frame at Waverley West, made by the Siemens General Electric Railway Signal Co. took control of the area. The HST is in platform 1, worked bi-directionally, and the Class 40 is on the North Loop Siding, which has since been removed following further track rationalisation because of electrification work.

Plate 142
When closure of the last section of the River-side branch took place on 11th September 1987, the only remaining traffic was to Shepherds scrap yard. Two years before the final train ran, Class 31/1 No. 31223 is seen on 1st April 1985 hauling 9P06, the St Peters to Tyne Yard trip working through Byker. The four (TOPS code) MDVs, destined for Lackenby and the POAs, for Tinsley, were all carrying scrap. The passenger service along this loop line had lingered until 23rd July 1973. Dmus had replaced the third-rail electric trains six years earlier.

This NE wood post slotted signal on the River-side branch was St Peters cabin No. 30 Down Main Distant (from the Newcastle direction). It had been modified with a LNER lamp (instead of the large ornate NE variety); a LNER flat-cap finial (replacing the McK&H parachute type), and an arm repeater (because it was sited round a corner out of sight of the signalman). **The signal became a fixed distant and the green glass from the lower spectacle was removed some years ago. The post also accommodated Malings Sidings No. 14 Down Main Starter at the top (the remains of Malings Sidings itself can be seen on the left). The tubular steel signal was the Up fixed Distant for Newcastle PSB No. 2 Up Riverside Home signal. Today, both signals and track have disappeared.**

Plate 143
New Holland Pier station and the connecting ferry service to Hull Corporation Pier closed on 25th June 1981, occasioned by the opening of the Humber Bridge. One month before closure, on 28th May, the extensive wooden structure was in a very dilapidated state as Class 114 dmu (cars 50043 and 56021 – since renumbered 53043 and 54021) – awaits departure with the 13.01 service for Cleethorpes.

New Holland Pier GF, a platform-mounted structure (to GC Type 5), housed a 12 lever, 6in centres, GC frame, and when new, boasted ten working levers. It controlled two platform lines and a Middle Siding, with engine release crossovers (part of one of which can just be seen in front of the dmu) to the Middle Siding, the course of which is still discernible. Although out of use, No. 7 ground disc signal (centre foreground) still guarded the outlet from the Middle Siding to the Platform Line.

Plate 144
Class 150/2 'Sprinter' No. 150226 with the 14.05 Sheffield to Hull service crosses the Goole Swing Bridge on 11th June 1988. Over the past years there have been several occasions when damage to this structure has cast doubts on the future of the Goole to Gilberdyke route. On 21st December 1973, the bridge was hit by a German coaster and normal services were not resumed until 7th October 1974. A decade later, in January 1984, "... due to the poor state of the bridge ...", BR recommended the route for closure and the threat was only withdrawn when Humberside County Council agreed to pay £1 million towards repairs. The latest serious incident occurred on 23rd November 1988, when a Swedish vessel almost knocked one of the fixed spans into the River Ouse.

Goole Swing Bridge was opened to traffic on 3rd July 1869, and the octagonal bridge control cabin shown here is regarded by BR as its oldest surviving operational signal box structure. Not originally a block post, it became a fully-fledged signal box in May 1933, when the cabins protecting the approaches to the swing bridge (Goole Bridge North and South) were closed, and the world's first relay interlocking control panel, controlling ten colour lights over a re-signalled area of 14 track miles, was installed in the bridge box. The signalling equipment was supplied by the Westinghouse Brake & Saxby Signal Co. Ltd to the design and specification of A.E. Tattersall, Signal & Telegraph Engineer, N.E. Area, LNER. The original panel (in a modified form) and the box are still extant. Note one of the overhead transmission line pylons above the rear vehicle.

Plate 145
On 22nd August 1981, the 09.22 (SO) Derby to Skegness train, headed by Class 20s Nos 20087 and 20070, is seen coming off the former GN route from Barkston East Junction. Hidden behind the second carriage were Class 31/1s Nos 31221 and 31216 waiting on the then recently singled loop from the "Joint" line, at Sleaford North Junction, heading a ballast working, awaiting access to the sidings. Within minutes and before the Class 31/1s had moved, Class 55 No. 55004 *Queen's Own Highlander* passed on the Up line heading the 09.54 (SO) Skegness to King's Cross service.

At the beginning of 1982, there were 17 surviving GN lower quadrant signals. This elevated shunt signal (one of only three) is of the "somersault" variety, developed as a result of the 1876 Abbots Ripton accident. Mounted on a concrete post, with a flat-cap finial, it is Sleaford West's No. 16 signal, controlling the exit from the Up Sidings and Cattle Dock to the double elevated shunt signals adjacent to the box (a GN brick Type 1 design of 1885 – note the tall chimney). Sleaford is incidentally one of the few places on BR still to have four cabins named after the cardinal points of the compass.

Plate 146
Unfitted freight services have become increasingly rare over recent years. One such working, the 9A66 Coed Bach Washery to Swansea East Dock train, approaches Kings Dock Junction on 7th August 1986. Headed by Class 37/0 No. 37236, it is composed of a rake of (TOPS code) MDV and MDO 21 tonne mineral wagons. (The use of unbraked MDO wagons ceased early in 1987.)

Kings Dock Junction survived until May 1987 when the box was closed and the remaining points and signals were recovered or converted to hand operation. A McK&H Type 3/Taff Vale Railway design of 1908, it received a new 100 lever GW frame in 1955. Latterly, it was owned and operated by Associated British Ports, who late in 1988, offered it free to any interested railway group. The tubular steel bracket signals were standard GW products, first introduced about 1943 when Scandinavian timber was in short supply. Rapid erection from prefabricated parts and reduced maintenance were the principal advantages of this functional design. The front of a two-way mechanical route indicator (left), and the rear of a five-way one (right) applying Down Dock Line to Down Loop (lever 66); Inwards Line (67); Down Tin Siding (68); Up Tin Siding (56); and Down No. 3 Line (69) can be seen. The stencil indications were stored out of sight in the lower portion of the apparatus, and when the signal was cleared, one was pushed up by a rod from the magazine into the glass screen, which was lit at night by a lamp.

Plate 147
The 13.40 Southport to Manchester Victoria train approaches Bolton on 11th August 1983 formed from a 'Calder Valley' 3-car set (Nos 51845, 59809 and 51824) and a Derby Lightweight 2-car set (Nos 53983 and 54266). Until recently this scene had been dominated by a lengthy footbridge, one abutment of which can still be seen to the right of the signal box. The bridge crossed the Lostock Junction lines and the long since lifted Johnson Street fork. This latter provided a direct connection between the Lostock Junction and the Blackburn lines.

Bolton West was one of the earliest installations of power operated points and signals in this country – and the first at a large passenger junction. Opened on 27th September 1903 in connection with the new station and situated within a triangle of lines, it replaced two mechanical cabins and cost £3,816. Originally, this 28ft by 12ft all-wood box, with its rare hipped roof peculiar to L&Y power boxes, had a ground floor entrance and internal staircase, but a new anti-blast brick wall base up to first floor level, and new outside entrance, was built during World War II. The cabin contained a miniature lever electro-pneumatic power frame of the Westinghouse Brake Company's Style B design – the General Arrangement drawings for which are numbered E65 and E66 and dated November 1898 and March 1899. The frame measured 18ft by 3ft 6in with the 83 levers spaced at 2½in centres. The point and signal motors were fed by compressed air at 65 lb psi, which accounted for the graceful movements of the signal arms. Bolton West closed on 8th December 1985, when a new PSB, this time with a Westinghouse panel controlling a revised track layout and colour light signals was commissioned.

Plate 148
Having first run on 1st August 1848, the "Irish Mail" is the oldest titled train in Britain. The morning Down service is seen hauled by Class 47/4 No. 47602 *Glorious Devon* as it descends into Holyhead on 26th August 1987. The locomotive was named at Exeter St Davids on 7th August 1985 as part of the GW 150 celebrations. The locomotive originally designated to carry the name – No. 47621 – had been named *Royal County of Berkshire* earlier in the summer.

Holyhead No. 38 signal – the Up Starter from Platforms 2 and 3 (centre foreground) survived in this form until February 1988. Its diminutive stature and short arm – perhaps the shortest on the LNW – were caused by its position and the resulting need to ameliorate its visibility under the road overbridge (see Plate 173) and to avoid the arm fouling the structure gauge of the adjacent Up Passenger Line (left). The push rod to the left of the solid pitch pine post, with galvanised iron cap, and the pressed steel arm, with its two distinctive corrugations to give rigidity, can be seen clearly in this "1883" standard design. It has been re-equipped as a limited clearance upper-quadrant signal after the spectacle casting broke and was brought back into use on 15th February 1988.

9 : Grouping Signal Boxes (1923-1948)

Plate 149

The pruning of services to the north and west of Manchester in the early 1960s led to the closure of Exchange station and the re-routing of the remaining services to Victoria on 5th May 1969. Twenty years later, much of this traffic now operates out of Piccadilly. The trans-Pennine service via Standedge was diverted from 15th May 1989. Dave Prescott (Provincial's Eastern Marketing Manager), said that the re-routing would " ... create many new journey opportunities ... " and " ... give easy access to south Manchester, Cheshire and the M6 corridor ... ". Before the change, Class 45/1 No. 45128 headed the 16.03 Liverpool to Newcastle train into Manchester Victoria on 18th April 1987. After withdrawal, this locomotive was resurrected in February 1989 to replace the ill-fated green liveried No. 45106. Unfortunately, potentially high repair costs, amongst other things, resulted in No. 45128 being returned to the scrap line.

The contract for the re-signalling of Victoria and Exchange stations was let in November 1927 to the then Westinghouse Brake & Saxby Signal Co. Ltd and finally completed in March 1929. Manchester Victoria West Junction is one of four LMS power boxes, which defy categorisation, but displays the 'art deco' style then in vogue. The design of the three Victoria cabins – Deal Street and Irwell Bridge Sidings were the other two – presented a difficult problem because of the limited space available, the line being mainly built on viaducts. A panelled brick base, in which there are some 3 x 2 ground floor windows, and a very large area of glazing on the operating floor, with three-panes high windows reaching to the overhanging flat-top roof, typified the design. Here the front windows have been renewed but the bay is original. West box contains a 95 lever Westinghouse Style K, 2½in centres, power frame, with miniature mechanical locking, placed at right angles to the track. The frame is number 33.

Plate 150 (Opposite)

On 3rd April 1986, Class 47/3 No. 47320 comes off the Southport line at Wigan Wallgate with 6H63, the 13.35 Appley Bridge to Northenden waste container empties. Opened in October 1982, Northenden was the second of four terminals to be built to cope with Greater Manchester's refuse. After passing through Wallgate station, the train will join the WCML and proceed to Hartford LNW Junction, before taking the ex-CLC route via Northwich and Skelton Junction.

Built to LMS ARP specifications, with 14in solid brick walls and a 12in thick reinforced-concrete flat roof, Wigan Wallgate was opened on 27th July 1941 to accommodate a 75 lever frame and a control panel with 38 switches. Based on the standard LMS ARP design, which omitted locking room windows and a roof canopy (see Plate 232), it incorporated some special features such as a different design of window (of prefabricated concrete), an overhanging canopy and, for some unexplained reason, especially at a time when censorship and security considerations demanded otherwise, concrete name panels, with large embossed letters placed centrally in the brickwork under the windows. They were quickly boarded over however and remained so until the war ended. Designated LMS Type 13+ and situated in the vee formed by the junction of the Up Liverpool (in front of the box) and Down Southport lines, 372 yards west of the station, Wigan Wallgate works to Parbold, Rainford and Warrington PSB.

Plate 151
Since the closure of Gateshead depot, a Crewe based fleet of 12 'dedicated' Class 47/4s has been responsible for "Trans-Pennine" services. However, frequent substitutions occur, and on 11th February 1989, Eastfield based Class 47/4 No. 47664 is seen rejoining the Up Main at Darlington South Junction with the 10.17 Newcastle to Liverpool Lime Street train. Note the 80ft communications tower on the station roof. It was one of five established by BR(NER) in 1964 and formed part of the first radio-telephone micro-wave link in the British Isles. It connects York, Darlington and Newcastle. For the purpose of amplification and redirection of the waves, towers were also constructed at Woolmoor (near Thirsk) and west of Ferryhill. The most northerly tower is in Tyne Yard, from where signals are maintained with Newcastle by means of co-axial cables.

The North Eastern Area of the LNER – one of three Operating areas, and certainly the most progressive in signalling terms - produced its first 'art-deco' cabin (at Thirsk) in 1933. The style varied widely in succeeding structures, although all were built of brick. Darlington, to LNER Type 12, exemplifies the 'pagoda' style (see Northallerton, Plate 167), with steeply-pitched hipped roofs, overhanging the upper floor windows, which have a horizontal glazing bar at waist height. When opened on 7th May 1939 as Darlington South, it contained a 155 lever, WB&SCo Style L power frame, positioned in the rear of the box. This particular equipment – a unique example on the NE Area – was ordered specifically so that a comparison, in terms of operating costs, maintenance and general performance, could be made between it and the Westinghouse Company's 'O.C.S.' panel interlocking installed at Northallerton. The power frame was replaced in June 1972 by a Westinghouse 'N-X' panel, the relays for which are housed in the single storey extension.

Plate 152
Class 37/0 locomotives replaced Class 27s on West Highland line passenger services in the summer of 1981. On 18th August 1984, Class 37/0 No. 37264 draws into Spean Bridge with the 09.50 Glasgow Queen Street to Fort William train. The locomotive was boasting the experimental livery that later became typical of the ScotRail Class 37s operating on the various Highland routes. Since the advent of RETB, Down trains now use the former Up platform and vice versa. This rearrangement, by no means peculiar to this station, makes access to the Departmental sidings much easier.

Soon after Mr A. E. Tattersall's appointment in 1943 as Assistant Chief Engineer (Signals), LNER, the Type 15 design for system-wide use appeared. Easily recognisable by their chamfered front (and sometimes rear) corners, and similarly shaped canopy, these cabins were constructed of brick (English Garden Wall bond on the Scottish Area ones), with concrete sills and lintels to the narrow horizontal locking room windows and large upper floor windows, with two horizontal glazing bars near the top and bottom. Until 1949, Spean Bridge boasted two cabins, one for the junction of the Fort Augustus branch, and one for the station. They were replaced by the present structure, situated on the Up platform, near its predecessor. It controlled the passing loop and goods yard with a 30 lever, RSCo. (Stevens pattern) frame, and was closed with the extension of RETB working from Banavie. Note the rodding run emanating from below the platform, and the signalman, who has just collected the key token for the single line section from Tulloch.

Plate 153
Following the electrification of the WCML north of Crewe, the majority of Class 50 locomotives were transferred to BR(WR). However, fifteen remained for use on non-electrified feeder routes such as Anglo-Scottish services between Liverpool/Manchester and Preston. One of this batch, No. 50035, did not reach Bath Road until January 1976. It is seen on 28th October 1988, approaching Paddington's platform 4 with the 12.00 departure from Oxford. The locomotive was named *Ark Royal* following a surprising BR press release in 1977. This stated that both Class 50 and 87 locomotives were to be given names "... providing an individual character for engines which were previously known by numbers only ...", thereby reversing the 1964 decision to discontinue naming.

Although closed as a block post under Stage 3 of the resignalling scheme on 29th October 1967, when Old Oak Common PSB took over control of the Down side of the station, Paddington Departure box still survives intact at the country end of platform 1. With the Arrival box, it was opened as part of the extensive track and power signalling works undertaken by the GW in 1933, when platforms 1 to 4 were arranged for departures, platforms 5 and 6 for both departures and arrivals, and platforms 7 to 12 for arrivals. Apart from the five other power boxes at Cardiff (1934) and Bristol (1935) – see *GWS* Plate 121 – and the ARP cabins, the GW built no modern style structures. Both the Arrival and Departure boxes, classified GW Type 18, had 14in thick brickwork, steel-framed operating floor windows, and reinforced concrete flat roofs. They contained GRSCo power frames, with draw slides instead of miniature levers, and mechanical locking.

Plate 154
On 31st July 1987, the 08.41 Bristol Temple Meads to Severn Beach service was a hybrid formation composed of a Class 121 single car (No. 55026) and the trailing vehicle of a Class 108 2-car set (No. 54207). The latter was a spare vehicle allocated to Bath Road (Unit B967) and had recently been transferred from Botanic Gardens. (It has since been matched with car No. 53622 and forms Unit B970). The Pressed Steel vehicle only made a brief sojourn at Bristol. Having arrived from Reading in May 1986, it was moved to Laira in October 1987 to help fill the gap caused by the transfer of Class 142 'Skippers' to Newton Heath and Heaton.

Just for a change, a rear view, which is often as interesting as a conventional front three-quarter one. The GW Type 28 design, introduced in 1900, as a gabled, cheaper version of the Type 27, was initially used only for temporary timber cabins and small break-section block posts. Noted for its longevity, this ubiquitous design originally sported vertical boarding, though most later examples had horizontal boarding (Type 28b). Opened in 1941 with a 46 lever frame, Holesmouth Junction latterly controlled access to the Port of Bristol Authority sidings (behind the dmu), until it was closed on 24th January 1988, together with Hallen Marsh and Avonmouth Goods Yard cabins, to which it worked AB. It was subsequently dismantled and has been re-assembled at the Birmingham Railway Museum, Tyseley.

Plate 155
Class 455/9 4-car emu No. 5910 leaves Waterloo with the 09.43 service for Windsor & Eton on 27th August 1988. The first Class 455s were delivered early in 1982 and commenced revenue earning service at the end of March. This set has since been adorned with the Network SouthEast livery that was introduced on 10th June 1986, when the London & South East sector was renamed. The original Class 455 units to be so treated were Nos 5850 and 5872.

Of the three BR boxes named Waterloo, the SR structure was by far the largest. Built almost entirely of concrete on the site of the old blacksmith's shop at the west side of the station throat, it was another one-off design, with a relay room and maintenance staff accommodation and facilities on the ground floor, and a control room above. From its opening on 18th October 1936 until 1984, it housed a 309 miniature lever WB&SCo all-electric Style L power frame – a type used extensively on the SR over a period of some 20 years – positioned in three separate sections for Main Local, Main Through and Windsor lines. A temporary small 'N-X' panel currently controls the station environs, until the area is subsumed by the new PSB at Wimbledon.

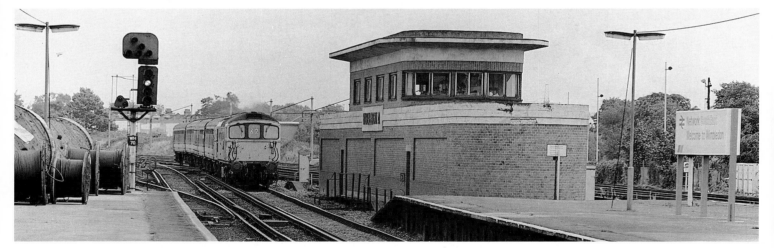

Plate 156
On 27th August 1988, Class 33/1 No. 33112 *Templecombe* approaches Wimbledon with the 12.10 Waterloo to Gillingham (Dorset) service. In October 1987, the locomotive was named to commemorate the reopening of the station which had previously closed in 1966. It was withdrawn on 7th October 1988 following a collision at Salisbury.

Marking the beginning of the SR's "streamline" period, the Type 13 design first appeared in the same year as Waterloo. It is arguably the most impressive of all 20th century box designs, with daring rounded corners to both the ground and operating floors, and the canopy. Nicknamed the "Glasshouse" style, it was buried during the Second World War, while the SR ARP Type 14 flourished, but was resurrected at Wimbledon (formerly named "A"), where steel frames replaced the earlier timber for the plate glass upper floor windows. Like the LMS Type 13+, the name was emblazoned on the front in embossed letters, 18 inches high. "Glasshouse" cabins contained either Style L power frames or, like Wimbledon, conventional mechanical lever frames, in this case, a 112 lever WB&SCo A2 frame. Opened on 29th February 1948, it works TCB to Clapham Junction "A", (signal box code WF – see Plate 159), Raynes Park (code WL), Wimbledon Park (code WBF) and Victoria PSB. Note the position 1 junction indicator, with only three lights, the style first adopted by the SR at Waterloo, astride WH70 signal (see Plate 164).

10 : Principles of Colour Light Signalling

Plate 157
Improvements are under way for the slow, albeit picturesque, Tyne Valley route. A £1 million investment is designed to increase line speeds to 70 mph. This follows the introduction of 'Super Sprinters' on Anglo-Scottish services in October 1988. However, 'Pacers' work most local trains and No. 143014 is leaving Bardon Mill on 6th February 1989 forming the 10.30 Newcastle to Carlisle.

The London underground railways pioneered colour light signalling in Great Britain early this century. The earliest and simplest types showed only two aspects: red/green and yellow/green. This multiple lens (or multi-unit) colour light distant signal on the Up Main at Bardon Mill displays yellow (in the lower lens) when at caution meaning "Be prepared to stop at next signal" and green (upper lens) when cleared meaning "Next signal showing a proceed aspect". It represents the colour light equivalent to the semaphore distant signal in Plate 16. All colour light signals carry an identification (or signal number) plate, generally consisting of one or two, but occasionally three – mainly on the BR(SR) – letters, referring to the signal box (or box code – see Plate 159). A one, two, three or four digit number corresponds to the controlling lever (in this case, No. 18) in the frame, or switch on the panel, in the signal box.

Plate 158
The future of Ilkley services has been in doubt several times since 1968, when their withdrawal was considered by the local Transport Users Consultative Committee (TUCC). Later, a proposal in 1972 to save on engineering work on the Baildon tunnels – located on the direct line between Shipley and Guiseley – involved the re-routing of the Bradford to Ilkley services via Apperley Junction where the trains would reverse. In 1985, all services in the area were threatened because the West Yorkshire Passenger Transport Executive could not meet spending restrictions imposed by the Government. However, the result was less dramatic: the number of trains to Ilkley was halved by terminating those starting from Bradford at Guiseley. During this unsettled time, on Easter Bank Holiday Monday 1987, Class 144 No. 144012 approaches Guiseley with the 13.40 Ilkley to Leeds service. On restarting, the train proceeded to Apperley Junction along the route singled as part of an economy measure in February 1983.

This standard two-aspect (red/green) multi-unit type of colour light signal (with the upper green bulb illuminated) is Guiseley's No. 15 Down Main Starting signal towards Ilkley. To the right of the green aspect, the letters ML are the trademark of the manufacturer of this particular type of signal head – M.L. Engineering Co. (Plymouth) Ltd – and bear no significance as far as railway operating is concerned. Opened in 1906, Guiseley box is a MR Type 3a design. Its lever frame was replaced by an IFS panel, with nine switches, controlling new colour lights, on 27th February 1983. The panel was extended to control the Up and Down Intermediate Block signals (see Plate 177) at Burley-in-Wharfedale on 8th May 1988, when two additional switches were provided.

Plate 159
After the opening of the North and South army camps in 1855, Ash Junction – renamed Ash on 1st December 1926 – became an important focus for military movements. In more peaceful times, on 17th August 1987, Class 421/2 (4-CIG) emu No. 1253, forming the 12.04 Guildford to Ascot service, is seen coming off the Ash spur, between Aldershot North and South Junctions, which connects the former SE and LSW lines. Electrified services on this route commenced on 2nd July 1939.

In 1926, the SR (South Eastern Division) initiated a letter coding system for signal boxes where colour light signals were installed, and FW was the code ultimately allotted to Ash Crossing. FW7 is a typical three-aspect multiple-unit lens colour light signal, equipped like most controlled colour light signals with a telephone communicating directly with the signal box. This is located in the black and white diagonal-striped cabinet lower down the signal post. To the right of the main signal lenses, miniature lenses, known colloquially by the train crews as "pig's ears", repeat the indications displayed in the main lenses. They were provided to enable the driver, who had brought his train to a stand close to the signal, to observe the aspect shown by the signal, and were another innovation first introduced at Waterloo. The box, opened on 13th February 1966 to BR(SR) Type 18 replacing an earlier structure, houses a Henry Williams, Darlington/Integra 'N-X' panel, made up of 26 x 12 tiles, working TCB to Guildford PSB (see Plate 207) and Wokingham.

Plate 160
Class 308/2 emu No. 308994 passes through Stanford-le-Hope with an eastbound ECS during the morning of 18th April 1984. These units entered service when the London, Tilbury & Southend line was electrified in June 1962. Specifically designed for work on the Tilbury boat trains, which had been diverted from St Pancras, they differ from other members of the class in having a Non-Driving Motor Luggage Van (MLV) in place of the Non-Driving Motor Brake Second Van (MBS).

Although the design concept differs from the multi-unit signals illustrated so far, this 3-aspect searchlight type colour light signal can display identical indications, red, yellow and green, by means of a moving mechanism within the signal head itself. Formerly controlled by lever 3, as indicated by the signal post identification plate, it has, since the closure of Stanford-le-Hope box on 19th May 1985, been replated PJ18 and worked remotely from Pitsea cabin some five miles away. Pitsea also supervises the level crossing by CCTV.

Plate 161
Class 423 (4-VEP) emu No. 7752 (since renumbered No. 3052) leaves Aldershot on 17th August 1987 with the 12.28 Alton to Waterloo service. Aldershot joined the network in 1870 when a line between Pirbright Junction and Farnham Junction was constructed. (The original Guildford to Alton line, opened in 1849, followed a course via Tongham and Ash Green.) Once the new route had been opened, passenger traffic on the Tongham route steadily diminished and the service was discontinued when the branch to Pirbright Junction was electrified on 4th July 1937.

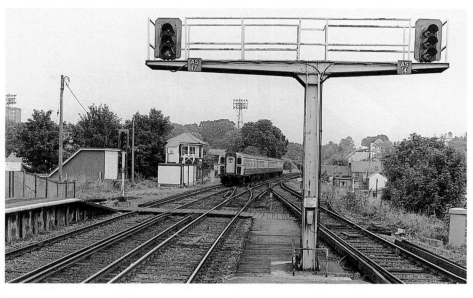

At Aldershot, the platform starting signals towards London are a mixture of 3 and 4-aspect multi-unit colour lights. The route from signal AS17 (the Down Main platform) is via the nearer trailing crossover, No. 8 points, while AS14 (from the Down Platform Loop) reads via No. 6 crossover, at the front of the train. A telephone, inside the cabinet (a black St Andrews cross on a white background) adjacent to the wooden barrow crossing, is provided to enable station staff to obtain the signalman's permission to cross the line in safety, (see Plate 243). Built to the LSW Type 4 design, the cabin, originally named Aldershot East, later "A", and now just plain Aldershot, contains a 4in centres, Stevens frame of 24 levers, all of which are in use. Block working is AB to Farnham and TCB to Ash Crossing and Ash Vale.

Plate 162
Even though Class 47/0 No. 47200 was promptly sent to the rescue, the failure on 25th August 1987, at Adlington of Class 87 No. 87022 *Cock o' the North,* while heading the 08.22 Euston to Manchester Piccadilly train, had a detrimental effect on subsequent services. After being held behind the express, Class 304 emu No. 304004 was running 40 minutes late as it left Kidsgrove with the 11.42 Manchester to Stoke-on-Trent working. As a result of flooding at Blythe Bridge, trains on the Crewe to Derby line were also dislocated. A shuttle service was operating between Crewe and Stoke using Class 108 dmus in place of the usual Class 150/1 'Sprinters'.

When engaged on maintenance duties in electrified areas, the S&T Engineer's staff are protected from the dangers of the OLE by wire mesh cages or screens on signals. Fitted with a screen, KC28, the Up Main Platform Starting signal towards Stoke, is a common example of a 4-aspect controlled colour light signal complete with a telephone. Replacing an older wooden cabin on the opposite side of the line, Kidsgrove Central is a BR(LMR) Type 15 box, with a 50 lever, BR(LMR) standard pattern frame. It was opened on Sunday, 25th July 1965, in connection with the introduction of MAS northwards to Macclesfield. TCB is worked to Crewe PSB, Mow Cop and Bradwell Sidings.

Plate 163
October 31st 1987 was a very dull autumn Saturday as Class 305/2 4-car emu No. 305515 pauses at Roydon with the 11.38 Liverpool Street to Bishops Stortford stopping service. The main building on the Down platform is now used as a restaurant and the booking office relocated on the Up platform in a much more modest modern structure. Electrified local services officially commenced on 21st November 1960. At first, trains from Liverpool Street worked via the Southbury Loop and divided at Broxbourne; one set was for Hertford and the other for Bishops Stortford.

This 4-aspect searchlight signal displays the same indications as the multi-unit examples seen at Aldershot and Kidsgrove. A second lens, showing yellow or nothing, has been added to a standard 3-aspect searchlight signal head (Plate 160), permitting the display of the double yellow indication meaning "Preliminary Caution or be prepared to find next signal showing one yellow light". Roydon No. 5 Up Main Second Home signal protects the MCB crossing and, when commissioned, used to control the entrance into the Up Goods Loop (see Plate 168). Dating from 1876, Roydon is the oldest GE/S&F Type 1 box still in use, and contains a reconditioned 27 lever McK&H frame, installed in 1959, in connection with the GE Line Electrification. It works TCB to Broxbourne (Plate 204) and Harlow Mill.

Plate 164
The first 'InterCity 125' service linking the "Granite City" with London commenced in October 1978. This view shows the 06.00 Aberdeen to King's Cross service approaching Durham on 3rd January 1986. Much has changed since this photograph was taken. During the first week of 1989, the Down Siding (the last track in the yard), was shortened to 100 yards. It only saw sporadic Departmental use after domestic coal deliveries ceased early in 1984. The Down platform has been lengthened and the car parking space (left) has been extended. As part of the ECML electrification, OLE was erected in the summer of 1989.

Nowadays, in normal circumstances, a passenger train driver is rarely required (except as in Plate 173) to pass a colour light signal at danger. At diverging junctions, and high-speed crossovers from Slow to Fast lines, and vice versa, only one signal is used with, above it, a junction indicator. This takes the form of a row of three (a few examples still exist only on the BR[SR]) or five white lights, projecting to the left at 45°, 90°, or 135° from the vertical (positions 1, 2 and 3) or right (positions 4, 5 and 6) depending on the number of routes reading from the signal. These white or lunar lights are extinguished when the signal is at danger, or when the principal high-speed route is set up, and are lit only when the diverging route is to be taken. Controlled from Tyne Yard PSB a TY369 signal, on the Down Slow at the north end of Durham station, is showing a green aspect and an illuminated junction indicator (Position 4) for the crossover from the Down Platform to the Down Fast. On Sunday 12th March 1989, this signal was repositioned 16 yards further north in connection with lengthening the Down platform.

Plate 165
The driver of 4M88, the 13.46 Southampton Maritime Container Terminal to Willesden Freightliner Terminal, awaits his relief at Eastleigh on 17th August 1987. The train is being hauled by Class 47/0 No. 47050, the first member of the class to be repainted in early Railfreight livery. Meanwhile, Class 423 (4-VEP) emu No. 7815 (since renumbered No. 3115) enters the station with the 13.42 Waterloo to Bournemouth service.

Eastleigh E93 signal is fitted with a two-way junction indicator (the lowest light being common to both) and reads three ways: with a green aspect only (as illustrated), the route from platform 2 is set straight ahead along the Up Slow towards Basingstoke, while with the right-hand (position 4) junction indicator illuminated and a proceed aspect, the route to the Up Main via No. 444 facing crossover in the foreground would be set up. The third route is the left-hand divergence (position 1 junction indicator) to Romsey and Salisbury, seen to the left of the signal telephone cabinet. Part of the 1966 Eastleigh PSB is visible to the left of the signs on the lamp post.

Plate 166
Class 47/4 No. 47557 draws to a halt at Manningtree on 28th August 1981 while heading the 12.21 Norwich to Liverpool Street train. Since the advent of a fully electrified service, these trains no longer call here. To the right of the locomotive, there are some (TOPS code) VDA vans forming part of the 6S96 Parkeston Quay to Mossend Speedlink service halted on the North Curve connecting Manningtree East and North Junctions.

Here at Manningtree, the Down Main Platform Starting colour light M197 is fitted with a position 4 junction indicator, which, when lit, reads to the right through the facing crossover to the left of the 25 mph PSR sign towards Harwich. M199 however applies to the bi-directional Up Main on which the train is approaching: with a proceed aspect only, it reads towards Harwich, and with the position 1 junction indicator lit, it reads through a trailing crossover behind the signal box towards Ipswich. Separate telephones, at the feet of the signal gantry, are provided for each signal.

Plate 169
Class 305/1 3-car emu No. 305401 leaves Hertford East on 22nd August 1987 with the 14.09 train for Liverpool Street. Electric services over the branch commenced in November 1960 and were routed via the five mile Southbury Loop which had been closed to regular passenger traffic since 1909.

In older installations, as at Hertford East, a single aspect subsidiary colour light may be used for the same purpose as that described in the previous plate. Two examples are visible below and off-set to the left of searchlight signals HE43 and HE44, and give access to the Carriage Washer Siding beyond and to the left of the box. Normally no light is exhibited (as illustrated) but when "off", a miniature yellow aspect is illuminated, the red light remaining lit. Note the wide-to-gauge trap points (below the cabin) provided to derail vehicles stabled on the Centre Siding in the event of a runaway. Built in 1887 by the GE to Type 7, the box contains a 45 lever McK&H frame and works TCB to Ware.

Plate 167 (Opposite, top)
In its declining years, Class 45/1 No. 45104 *The Royal Warwickshire Fusiliers* became somewhat of a celebrity when Tinsley depot lined the windows and grills in silver and made replacement nameplates. It is seen approaching Northallerton on 3rd March 1987, heading the 11.24 Newcastle to Liverpool Lime Street train. 'Peaks' first appeared on the 'trans-Pennine' route at the beginning of the 1962 winter timetable and continued to give frequent and reliable service for over 25 years. The Down platform was formerly an island with a bay for the Wensleydale branch trains, which used the now uplifted single line curve to Castle Hills Inner Junction, diverging beyond the milk depot. The bridge (adjacent to the depot) marks the point where the Up and Down Longlands Loop lines pass under the ECML.

Placed directly below the red aspect of Northallerton N54 signal is a position light subsidiary signal. It has only an "off" aspect, consisting of two white lights at an angle of 45°, in the upper left-hand quadrant. No "on" aspect is shown (ie the lights are extinguished) because the instruction to stop is already given by the red aspect in the running signal (as illustrated). When "off", the subsidiary signal indicates to the driver that he may draw ahead at slow speed beyond the main red aspect for shunting purposes only, but may not pass any other signal at Danger. It used to apply along the Down Main line towards Darlington, or with the right-hand junction indicator lit, via No. 212 facing crossover points to the Down Northallerton Loop line towards Teesside. The signalling from here to Darlington was installed by the WB & S Co and Northallerton box was opened the day war was declared on Germany - Sunday, 3rd September 1939.

Plate 168 (Opposite, bottom)
Electrification of the section between Shepreth Branch Junction and Roydon coincided with the reintroduction of through services between Cambridge and King's Cross. (Through trains, such as the "Cambridge Buffet Car Express", last ran on the Great Northern route when the Outer Suburban electrification was inaugurated on 7th February 1978.) During the decade when all through services to Cambridge worked out of Liverpool Street, Class 86/2 No. 86233 *Laurence Olivier* heads through Brimsdown with the 15.00 ex-Kings Lynn service on 22nd August 1987.

A position light subsidiary signal may also be used to authorise direct entry from a running line via facing connections to a goods loop, yard, siding or "No Block" line. Below and off-set to the right of the red aspect of Brimsdown BD7 is a subsidiary signal which, when cleared, reads to the Up Sidings (North) seen to the right of the locomotive, via No. 13 facing crossover (in the foreground) and No. 25 trailing points (out of sight below the fifth coach). Brimsdown cabin was rebuilt in 1944 following bomb damage, and now houses a 37 lever McK&H, 4in centres frame plus a BR York-built 'N-X' panel, commissioned on 20th March 1988. TCB is worked to Hackney Downs, Stratford, South Tottenham and Cheshunt Junction.

Plate 170

In 1978 BR spent £500,000 on the maintenance and restoration of Hull Paragon's overall roof, which forms such an impressive backdrop to this photograph. (It is unfortunate that rationalisation has left two spans covering a car park rather than tracks!) On 30th May 1984, an immaculate Class 31/4 No. 31441 leaves with the 15.50 service to Lancaster, while the two Class 31s in the station are at the head of the 16.01 Sheffield and the 16.38 Leeds trains. The use of locomotives and stock on these routes was discontinued the following October to enable the Provincial Sector to reduce costs in line with the smaller Public Service Obligation (PSO) grant.

The ground position light shunt signal conveys the same meanings as the shunting disc signal in Plate 25. Having three miniature lights arranged in a triangle, it shows one red (bottom left) and one white light (bottom right) for the normal or "on" position; when cleared, the red light is extinguished and the second white light at the top is lit. The red lens may be replaced by a yellow one where a shunting signal may be passed at danger (see Plate 27). The first colour light re-signalling of Hull Paragon was completed on 24th April 1938, when a WBS&Co. "O.C.S." route setting panel, with 230 possible routes, was brought into use. This panel was retired to the NRM, York, in December 1984, when Hull was again re-signalled and the track layout considerably simplified.

Plate 171

On 4th August 1981, Class 40 No. 40154 takes the Leith branch at Portobello Junction. Heading 6S41, the 09.05 Haverton Hill to Leith South ICI company train, which conveys anhydrous ammonia, it has, since 1985, run overnight and the short wheelbase wagons were replaced by high capacity bogie tanks in June 1984. Between 1985 and 1988, Leith was also serviced by 6S44 from Immingham, which replaced 6S41 on several days a week.

Where a ground position light (or sub) signal applies to more than one route, up to a maximum of six stencil route indicators, corresponding to the number of routes available with each showing a figure or letter, are mounted above the sub. At Portobello Junction, which was remodelled as a ladder junction in October 1987, No. 852 sub reads two ways, from the East Depot Line to either the Down/Up Suburban Lines (a single line at this place, extreme right) or the Up/Down Millerhill single line, adjacent to it. The rear of another ground sub with double route indicator can be seen to the left of the picture. Maximum dimensions are 430 mm wide by 410 mm high.

Plate 172
On 20th June 1987, Class 47/4 No. 47497 approaches Newcastle Central hauling the empty stock from Heaton Carriage Sidings that will later form the 12.25 departure to Liverpool. The W, X, Y and Z Goods Lines, as well as the AB Sidings (extreme right), which formerly allowed freight workings to avoid the station, were truncated at the beginning of 1989. This was to allow the Provincial Sector to construct a new island platform which was partly brought into operation on 18th November 1989, when platform 16 was opened to the public.

In older installations of colour light signalling (such as Newcastle, commissioned on 12th April 1959), it was then the practice to provide two ground subs, one mounted above the other to differentiate between two routes. Like the ground discs in Plate 30 the top sub of N136 applies to the left-hand route, in this case from A B Sidings to the Shunt Spur (buffer stops), while the lower sub reads to X Goods Line N116 signal. The back of another double sub signal (N107) is visible below the rear bogie of the Class 47. In 1959, there were 131 sets of points including 13 movable diamonds, operated by compressed air supplied to the points through a 2in main, from two compressor stations, one at the east, the other at the west end of the signalling area.

Plate 173
On 26th August 1987, the late arrival of the S.S. *Columba* on the connecting ferry service from Dun Laoghaire, slightly delayed the 12.55 departure for Euston. It is seen 17 minutes "down" headed by Class 47/4 No. 47590 *Thomas Telford* getting to grips with the 1 in 90 climb out of Holyhead (the severest gradient on the North Wales coast).

Above the HD113 identification plate is a draw-ahead position light subsidiary signal, which is not normally lit, since the colour light above always displays either a red (as in the picture) or yellow aspect. It is the colour light equivalent of the signal shown in Plate 23, and has the same meanings. When the two white lights (known unofficially by drivers as "cat's eyes") are lit for proceed, a driver is authorised to pass the main aspect at red and, with no route indication, to proceed for shunting purposes, but not pass any other signal at danger. Three stencil route indicators are mounted above the draw-ahead and with a route indication, say WP for Washing Plant line, it permits a train to go towards the next stop signal (or buffer stop, where there is no signal in advance) into an already occupied section of track, prepared to stop short of any obstruction. The 4-way stencil indicator on the extreme right shows the amount of space available in whichever Depot siding a train is being shunted. When new in 1937, Holyhead had a 115 lever LMS standard 4½in centres frame.

Plate 174
Two 3-car Class 503 emus (Nos 28385, 29839 and 29152 + 29134, 29844 and 28378) draw into Bidston on 23rd April 1984, forming the 11.07 West Kirby to Liverpool Loop service. The station has had a chequered career. After opening on 2nd July 1866, the whole line was closed on 8th July 1870, and on re-opening on 1st August 1872, the station still had no distinct *raison d'être* and was closed again in June 1890. Five years later, a line to Seacombe was opened and in 1896 the North Wales & Liverpool Railway joined the Wirral Railway at Bidston, resulting in the second re-opening in May. Today, besides being an interchange between the Merseyrail electrics and the dmu service to Wrexham, it serves Noctorum, a large "overspill" development along the Fender Valley and an "out-of-town" shopping complex on Bidston Moss.

Stencil route indicators are rarely used in conjunction with main running colour light signals, except when speeds are low. Departing trains from Bidston station receive one of two route indications with No. 12 signal cleared, depending on their destination, the left-hand one towards Wrexham (15 mph PSR) and the right-hand one via the trailing crossover (10 mph PSR) towards West Kirby. Like Holyhead, Bidston Dee Junction box is a LMS Type 11c design, dating from the late 1930s, and contains a 65 lever frame installed in 1952.

Plate 175
On 3rd September 1987, Class 20s Nos 20140 and 20078 approach Leeds City with refurbished Mark III stock from Derby, destined for Neville Hill depot. The erection of OLE – energised on 4th July 1988 – has since transformed this scene.

Again, where speeds are low, at the approach to and exit from large stations for example, a theatre type or multi-lamp route indicator, showing a letter, number or sometimes a combination of both, formed by a lamp display, is employed (see Plate 219). Consisting of a square frame with a lunar white front cover glass screen, mounted adjacent to the signal to which it applies, it is capable of showing up to ten or more different characters. No indication is shown when the main signal is at danger. Sometimes, as at Leeds, double-sided indicators are used, where a long train may have to stand beyond the platform starting signal. The rear facing indicator has an amber coloured cover glass to attract the driver's attention, to avoid any confusion with drivers of incoming trains, and/or to warn men working on the track. Leeds was last re-signalled in 1967.

Plate 176
Following the closure of Lincoln depot, the majority of the Class 114 dmus were withdrawn. Some of the survivors were converted to parcels sets and operated from Cambridge, whilst the remainder were reallocated to Birmingham. Approaching Worksop on 27th May, 1987 with the 14.02 Lincoln to Sheffield service are cars 54011 and 53030. They were transferred on 4th October 1987 and became Tyseley set TS230. It was withdrawn on 15th May 1989.

Situated 28 yards from the MCB crossing, Worksop East No. 4 Up Main Home 3-aspect colour light, placed on a right-hand bracket post (to avoid obstructing the platform) was commissioned on 1st February 1981. To improve the sighting of the signal, an adjacent 3-aspect colour light co-acting signal, plated WE4 Co-actor, was provided between the Up and Down lines, at ground level, the red aspect being uppermost. Worksop East is a MS&L Type 2 design of about 1880, and contains a 20 lever frame and small switch panel.

Plate 177
After being singled as a result of the 1963 Beeching Report, the reinstatement of the $23\frac{1}{2}$ miles of double track between Blair Atholl and Dalwhinnie took place during 1976/77. The £4 million investment was a result of the substantial increases in passenger and freight movements related to North Sea oil developments. Descending from Druimuachdar Summit on the relaid section, the 10.15(SuO) Inverness to King's Cross "Highland Chieftain" service, passes Dalanraoch on 5th June 1988. This train commenced ten years after "The Clansman" was inaugurated on 6th May 1974. The introduction of a daytime service between London and the Highland Capital coincided with the completion of electrification between Euston and Glasgow.

When intermediate signal boxes, controlling nothing more than say home and distant signals for each line and sited between junction or station cabins, began to be abolished because of rising costs in staffing them, IB signals were sometimes installed to keep the even spacing of the block sections. This arrangement is akin to an additional starting signal with its own distant, replacing those worked from a cabin. It thus preserves track capacity by allowing two trains in the enlarged block section, separated by the IB home signal. Years ago, conventional semaphore signals, controlled from the box in rear, were used but nowadays colour lights have superseded them. Identifiable by its white plate with vertical black band, Blair Atholl's No. 32 Down IB 2-aspect (red/green) home signal at Dalanraoch protects the trailing crossover, controlled from Dalnacardoch ground frame (see Chapter 11) just beyond the bridge. The resignalling of the Highland main line, and the restoration of double track between Blair Atholl and Dalwhinnie was the subject of a detailed article in "Modern Railways" for March 1980.

Plate 178
On 1st July 1984, Class 40 No. 40009 heads 4M19, the 13.30 Heaton Carriage Sidings to Manchester Red Bank newspaper empties, past Eryholme, five miles south of Darlington. This locomotive was the last vacuum braked Class 40 to remain in service and was withdrawn four months later. In 1988, the contract to carry newspapers was not renewed and the last train ran on 10th July.

D38 is an example of a 4-aspect semi-automatic searchlight signal. Its white enamelled identification plate with horizontal black band indicates that it can work as either an ordinary automatic signal, or a controlled signal, worked from the ground switch panel controlling the power-worked emergency crossover connections at Eryholme. The history of these plates is of interest: the LNER (North Eastern Area) lettered their automatic signals D or U (for Down or Up) and numbered them according to their mileage from a specific place. Thus D38 is 38+ miles from York on the Down Main. It has since been replaced by the 4-aspect multi-unit signal seen crossed out of use. On the extreme left, note the former Eryholme box, closed in January 1977, now a relay room.

11 : Ground Frames

Plate 179
The station staff come to the rescue when the locomotive crew have difficulties in operating the Bridgwater Station Ground Frame. Having arrived 'light', Class 47/3 No. 47330 crosses from the Down Main to the Up Main to gain access to the sidings prior to heading 6M34, the 17.40 (TO) United Kingdom Fertilisers (UKF) service for Ince on 28th July 1987.

Where a remote siding or crossover exists at a place which exceeds the 350 yards limit for the mechanical operation of points from a signal box, what is known as a GF is provided. Often out in the open at the site of the connections it controls, a ground frame consists of a scaled-down version of a signal box lever frame, and can contain any number of levers, (typically however three or four is the norm), for the points, lock bars (and sometimes shunting signals) under its jurisdiction. Locking all the other levers normal, the ground frame release lever, when normal, is itself locked or released either mechanically, by an Annett key (named after its inventor, James Annett), issued by the signalman at the supervising signal box, or electrically by a lever or, as in this case, a switch in the governing PSB. Bridgwater Station GF is released from Bristol PSB and controls a facing crossover and facing points leading to a nest of sidings west of Bridgwater station. It had been intended in June 1988 to replace it by an electric ground switch panel, controlling clamplock power points, with no alteration to existing associated signals, but the work was postponed.

Plate 180
When this photograph was taken on 20th August 1983, the section between Gannow Junction and Hall Royd Junction was under threat of closure. Subsequently the line was reprieved and a new local passenger service was introduced between Preston and Leeds in October 1984. At the same time, the few remaining locomotive hauled summer Saturday trains were discontinued. During the last season of these workings, Class 37/0 No. 37046 mounts Copy Pit Summit with the 13.59 (SO) Blackpool North to Sheffield train.

Often a GF (but nowadays, particularly in MAS areas, a small switch panel) is provided at a remote location where main to main emergency crossover points are needed for use when SLW necessitated by engineering operations, etc., takes place. Here, at Copy Pit Summit, a three lever Emergency GF, released from Preston PSB, controls a facing crossover, over which a 20 mph PSR is in force. Situated on the Down side of the East Lancashire line at 26 miles 22 chains from Farington Curve Junction, it was brought into use on 21st October 1973 under Stage C of the East Lancashire line Resignalling Scheme. The existing trailing crossover, (below the leading coach), controlled by No. 12 lever in the former Copy Pit cabin (right), is now power-worked and signalled from Preston PSB. Note that almost every GF has a telephone to its supervising box.

12 : A Power Scheme – Doncaster in Transition

Plate 181
A late morning scene bustling with activity at the north end of Doncaster on 26th July 1977. The main working is the departing 08.00 King's Cross to Edinburgh service hauled by Class 55 No. 55022 *Royal Scots Grey,* while Class 40 No. 40118 propels the empty stock off the 08.53 ex-Cleethorpes out of platform 1. The Class 114 dmu (left) is stabled; that in bay platform 7 is waiting to depart with the 10.39 local service to Leeds. At platform 3b, a Class 101 dmu forms the 08.02 Scarborough to Manchester Piccadilly train (via Bridlington and Hull). Behind the Anglo-Scottish express leaving from platform 4, a Class 104 dmu has arrived with the 09.51 Sheffield to Cleethorpes working.

Doncaster was the site chosen for the debut of a revolutionary development in control panel technology, called sequence-switch interlocking. Conceived before World War II and developed by A.E. Tattersall, whose visionary ideas of the late 1920s and early 1930s propelled British signalling practice well and truly forward into the electrical era. This unusual route-setting system used rotary thumb switch handles, of the type then employed in some systems of automatic telephone working. The fact that each switch, which dealt with up to eleven conflicting routes, could not be in two positions at once, provided natural interlocking between routes. It therefore greatly reduced the number of relays needed and consequently the size and cost of the boxes. It was ironic that Tattersall of all men was compelled against his wishes by the Operating Superintendent, Southern Area, LNER to install two control panels in separate boxes, North (shown here) and South. They proved remarkably reliable in service and were supplied by STC, while the searchlight signals and electric point machines were the products of the GRSCo.

Plate 182
Two generations of 'InterCity' travel and signalling stand in contrast at the south end of Doncaster station on 5th August 1979. The HST is forming the 10.15 (SuO) Aberdeen to King's Cross train while Class 55 No. 55018 *Ballymoss* arrives with the 14.05 (SuO) King's Cross to York semi-fast service.

Thirty years' development in signal box styles of architecture: the new PSB, situated south of the station on the Up side and built by a local building contractor, J. Dixon (Doncaster) Ltd, to the design and specification of the Eastern Region Architect, sits opposite the LNER-designed Doncaster South box. It housed the other sequence-switch interlocking panel, brought into service in January 1949, and closed on 8th July 1979, when Stage 1 of the PSB was commissioned. Its Westinghouse 'N-X' control panel replaced 51 mechanical and two power boxes, covering 155 route miles (73 on the ECML between Stoke Tunnel [north end] and Shaftholme), and worked to 15 fringe boxes. Nine MCB, 24 CCTV controlled crossings, and 12 AHB were included in the scheme, which had 1,115 track circuits and 42,145 relays. Much of the equipment installed at the time was a.c. immune in readiness for proposed electrification. Judged by late 1980s' technology however, it is now out of date!

Plate 183

On 30th May 1979, Class 37 No. 37119 pauses alongside the station with an eastbound trip working awaiting a path across the ECML to gain the Scunthorpe line. The train is composed of a mixture of 26 tonne hoppers (HJV), 16 tonne mineral wagons (MCV), 'Covhops' (CCV), bogie bolsters (BEV) and 'Presflos' (PCA). The locomotive, in fact, is none other than the prototype Class 37 (ex-No. D6700). Parked on the right is one of the now extinct Class 123 dmus which spent their last years on Manchester Piccadilly–Sheffield–Hull/Cleethorpes services.

Until the 1949 re-signalling, the main line cabins in the station area were "A" and "B", and Doncaster "C", to the north west of the station, was a relic of that era. Only five of the 42 levers were spare from 1949, and complicated signalling arrangements, using control, release and acceptance levers between Doncaster North and South existed. The train was photographed on the Down GN Goods Independent, about to pass 37-40 signal. To the left, the Down SY (South Yorkshire) Goods Independent has been severed at 28-31 signal, and the Up SY Goods Independent has been completely lifted in connection with track remodelling and rationalisation. Doncaster "C" was closed on 16th September 1979.

Plate 184

In April 1979, all Haymarket and Gateshead allocated 'Deltics' were transferred to York. Only weeks after this move, on 1st June 1979, ex-BR(ScR) Class 55 No. 55019 makes a spirited departure past Bridge Junction heading the 12.15 York to King's Cross semi-fast service. This locomotive had the distinction of being the last member of the class to be named. In a ceremony at Glasgow on 11th September 1965, it was christened *Royal Highland Fusilier*. The original plan had been to name the Haymarket allocation after birds!

Bridge Junction box, a GN Type 1/Decoy design, situated on the Down side, 155 miles 38 chains from King's Cross, worked to Doncaster South (588 yards north) and Balby Junction (326 yards south). It contained an 85 lever frame and closed on 8th July 1979. This photograph from Balby Bridge, clearly shows some of the modernisation work in progress: to the left, the Down Goods No. 1 and No. 2 lines have been replaced by a new single line bi-directional curve, known as the Up/Down Hexthorpe Goods; the carriage sidings, behind the box, have been lifted, and to the right of the 'Deltic', the new Up Slow D268 signal has already been erected. Several arms of semaphore signals have been removed, but the 1949 vintage colour lights, worked from Doncaster South box, protecting the Up Slow-Up Main connection, still survived.

Plate 185
A Derby built Class 114 2-car dmu approaches Doncaster on 29th May 1980, with the 12.25 stopping service from Leeds. It boasts the short lived – and rather boring – white livery, that was originally applied in June 1974 to the refurbished 3-car Class 101 set (Nos 51451, 59551 and 51518). This was the first real break from the all-over blue livery since green had been discontinued in the mid 1960s.

Although built on the former West Riding & Grimsby Railway (a partnership of the GN and GC companies), Bentley Crossing was a GN designed cabin. It was situated on the Down side of the line, 1 mile 856 yards from Doncaster North and 2 miles 164 yards from Skellow. Latterly, it worked AB on the Up Main and TCB on the Down Main to Doncaster North, and TCB to Skellow (see Plate 186). All its points and semaphore signals had been removed some years ago, leaving only three of the 18 levers of the S&F frame in use: these were No. 18 Barrier Release lever, and Nos 2 and 14, the Up and Down Home colour light signals, protecting the MCB crossing, installed on 23rd July 1978. Like Little Mill, it was converted to CCTV operation, on 7th December 1980, when the cabin was closed and Doncaster PSB took over control.

Plate 186
On 28th August 1980, an unidentified Class 47 locomotive makes slow progress as it comes off the short connection from Carcroft Junction and passes Skellow Junction with an mgr service from Brodsworth Colliery to Thorpe Marsh Power Station.

This view of Skellow on the Stainforth leg of the West Riding & Grimsby Railway, looking west towards Leeds, shows its position at the eastern apex of a triangular complex of junctions. It used to control the extensive network of sidings of Bullcroft Colliery (now the site of the factory and car park), and the 1916-built spur (off the right of the picture) to the Hull & Barnsley Railway main line

at Bullcroft Junction. This demanded a new signal box (to GN Type 4b), which for many years faced its older sister across the junction. From 8th March 1970, both Carcroft and Adwick cabins (at the south and west corners of the triangle, on the Doncaster–Leeds route) were closed, their areas being controlled from a panel in Skellow. It succumbed on 16th August 1981 to Doncaster PSB, which then linked up with Leeds PSB.

Plate 187
An HST screams past Shaftholme with the 11.35 King's Cross to Newcastle service on 29th May 1980. The junction is located 4 miles north of Doncaster. Until the NE line from Shaftholme Junction, through Selby to York was brought into use on 2nd January 1871, traffic on the ECML went by way of Askern Junction, Knottingley and Church Fenton.

Shaftholme box, situated in the vee of the ECML and the L&Y to Knottingley (on the left behind the bushes), replaced an earlier GN cabin in 1958. It was originally equipped with a 35 lever frame, but latterly a switch panel had been installed. Before closure on 26th October 1980, it worked TCB to Selby panel box and Bentley Colliery on the ECML; TCB to Applehurst Junction on the NE curve; and AB to Askern (see Plate 188) on the L&Y line. The building still survives however to house one of the thirteen local control panels associated with the Doncaster PSB scheme.

Plate 188
On 29th May 1980, in the days before the Class 56s took over power station workings, Class 47/3 No. 47308 drifts through Askern with a train of (TOPS code) HEA empties from Drax. The mgr principle was one strongly advocated by Dr Beeching in the early 1960s. Many of the HAA hoppers used in these operations today are now around 25 years old.

Between 1870 and 1890, the L&Y used five leading signalling contractors to build its cabins. Askern, a BTF, RSCo. design of the late 1880s still carrying a cast iron "Beware of the Trains" sign, worked AB to Shaftholme and Norton boxes. Its original L&Y frame was replaced in 1959 when a McK&H No. 16 pattern, 21 lever frame and gate wheel was installed. The cabin was closed under the Doncaster scheme on 26th October 1980, when the newly-built Norton gate box took over control of the lifting barriers by means of CCTV.

Plate 189
A Class 31 locomotive approaches Kirk Sandall Junction on 29th May 1980, and prepares to enter the Rockware Sidings with
8E08, the 10.11 from Wallerscote. Composed of gunpowder vans (TOPS code) CXV and CHV 'Covhops', the train had earlier worked
to Stainforth Junction to allow the locomotive to run-round.

**The two signal brackets situated 181 yards east of Kirk Sandall box were shorn of their arms on 17th February 1980, when the cabin
was closed and control was transferred to Doncaster PSB. Reading from left to right, the signals were No. 42 Down Main Home; No. 26
Down Main Home to Down Goods; No. 31 Down Main Home to Up Branch (the South Yorkshire Joint line via Low Ellers to Dinning-
ton and beyond); No. 37 Down Goods Home to Down Main; No. 47 Down Goods Home; and No. 46 Down Goods Home to Up Branch.
Only four pairs of points, worked by BR-designed, electro-hydraulic 'clamp-lock' machines, remain at the junction today. One of the
boxes housing the points mechanism can be seen below the locomotive's battery box.**

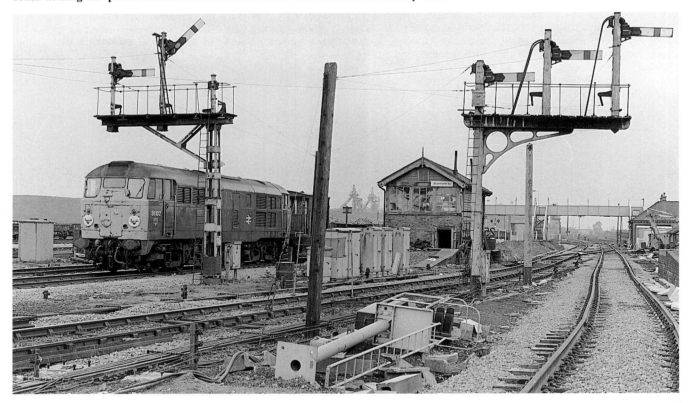

Plate 190
Signalling and track renewals continue on 29th May 1980 as Class 31/1 No. 31102 passes through Stainforth & Hatfield with empty
wagons from the Civil Engineer's sidings at Barnetby.

**The three-arm GC bracket (with more modern upper quadrant arms and fittings), carried the Down Goods Home signals to Down
Skellow (No. 60 left); to Down Main (No. 64); and to Down Goods (No. 68). It was replaced by the colour light signal (No. D641),
lying in the foreground, on 29th June 1980, when Stainforth cabin was closed and control transferred to Doncaster PSB. Hatfield Colliery winding gear can be seen to the left of the box, whose 95 levers were reduced to 77, to make space for a 'N-X' panel, which
controlled Thorne Junction, 1 mile 51 chains to the east, from 4th June 1972. Note the pennant below the guard's van indicating an
Engineer's possession of the Down Goods line.**

Plate 191
Although scheduled to travel via Gainsborough Central, Class 37/0 No. 37252 passes the semi-derelict Kirk Sandall Junction cabin on 29th May 1980 with 6E60, the 11.05 Preston Docks to Lindsey Oil Refinery tank empties. The Up (next to the cabin) and Down Goods lines between here and Bentley Junction had been taken out of use but were still in situ pending removal.

This view, turning through 180° from Plate 189, shows the second box at Kirk Sandall, opened on 18th June 1916, with the quadrupling of the line from Doncaster to Thorne Junction. It was constructed on the east side of the line, some three miles from Doncaster station, to a GC timber Type 5 design, and measured 30ft by 12ft. Its 48 lever, 4½in pitch frame, erected by McK&H, controlled a complicated junction, with crossovers from both Down and Up lines in both directions and connections to works premises spanning the running lines. Latterly, it worked to Bentley Junction and Stainforth cabins (AB on the Main Lines; PB on the Goods Lines), and EKT to Markham Sidings box on the single line South Yorkshire Joint branch.

Plate 192
Fresh from an intermediate repair at Doncaster Works, Class 55 No. 55019 *Royal Highlander Fusilier* makes good progress through Stainforth & Hatfield station with the 12.05 King's Cross to Hull service on 29th May 1980. Even though HSTs had been a regular sight for thirteen years, Hull dispatched a locomotive hauled SuO service for the capital until 1st October 1989. This was the last regular ECML passenger service to take a diesel locomotive into King's Cross.

Taken from the station footbridge, this view towards Doncaster (in the opposite direction to Plate 190), shows on the extreme left, the new relay room, housing another of the local control panels. The connections between the Down Goods, the Down Main and the Skellow line can be seen below the steel bracket carrying the Down Main Third Home signals. To the right of No. 62 (to Doncaster) at clear is No. 59 (to Skellow), while No. 63 (to Doncaster via the Down Goods) has had its arm removed.

Plate 193
While working the 15.30 Cleethorpes to Sheffield local train on 28th August 1980, a Class 105 2-car dmu passes Hexthorpe Junction's sole surviving semaphore signal. To the left is the route to Bentley Junction, allowing freight services for Humberside to avoid conflicting movements on the ECML north of Doncaster station.

Hexthorpe Junction was a standard GC Type 5 box, measuring 37ft by 12ft. The brickwork surrounding the ground floor was built, as noted elsewhere, as protection from possible enemy action during World War II. The box contained a 70 lever frame, controlling the junction of the GC Doncaster Avoiding Line (to the left of the cabin), with the Doncaster to Sheffield line. It was closed on 31st August 1980, when Doncaster and Sheffield PSBs finally met up.

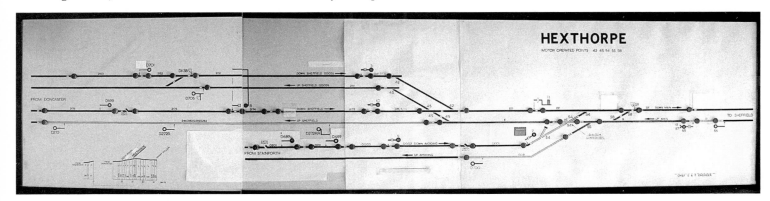

Plate 194
When this photograph was taken on 28th August 1980, considerable stage-work had altered the signalling and layout, as indicated by the number of paper amendments affixed to the signal box diagram. By this time, TCB working to Doncaster PSB and Stainforth (on the Avoiding Line) was in operation, but AB to Cadeby Colliery cabin (towards Sheffield) still remained in use.

Plate 195
Part of the 70 lever, GC frame at Hexthorpe. In this particular type of frame, the levers are spaced at intervals of $4\frac{1}{2}$in (or $4\frac{1}{2}$in pitch or centres). They are painted according to the functions they perform: stop signals – red; distant signals – yellow; points – black; locking bars – blue; spare levers – white, and so on. Levers 60, 63 and 64 are spare and have had their description plates removed. Power-worked points, painted blue/black, and colour light signals have short-handled levers, which thereby remind the signalman that there is no need for great physical effort to pull them. The lever collar on No. 60 is a safety reminder appliance used by signalmen in the circumstances described in Plate 19. The mechanical interlocking, achieved by a system of tappets and rods attached to the lower part of the lever frame below floor level in the locking room, is to a design unique to each signal box. It prevents a signalman from setting up two conflicting routes and ensures that signals can be cleared only when the points to which they apply are correctly set and locked.

13 : British Railways Signal Boxes

Plate 198
In February 1985, BR decided to break with the Rail Blue livery which prevailed for two decades. Railfreight adopted the grey livery that had been applied to the newly constructed Class 58 locomotives. Class 47/3 No. 47368 boasted these colours when it was photographed passing Vitriol Works on 15th August 1988, heading 6M54, the 10.15 Leeds Shell Sidings to Stanlow empty 100 tonne oil tanks.

The BR(LMR) Type 14 design was built of brick (Flemish bond being common) with rectangular concrete locking room windows and flat reinforced concrete roofs. An external concrete-stepped staircase, not visible in this view of Vitriol Works box, was combined with a large extension, which housed the toilet, etc. Situated on the Up side a few yards south of the older box it replaced, Vitriol Works was opened in 1954 to work inter alia connections to the then new Chadderton Power Station – sidings to the right, behind the cabin. It was equipped with a 65 lever, BR(LMR) standard frame of which originally only seven levers were spare. Today, the block sections are to Thorpes Bridge Junction and Castleton East Junction. Note the original BR(LMR) enamel nameboard.

Plate 196 (Opposite, top)
The 17 miles between Aberystwyth and Dovey Junction is the longest single line section on the present day Cambrian network. On 1st August 1987, Class 150/1 'Sprinters' Nos 150148 and 150128 reach the end of this stretch while forming the 13.30 Aberystwyth to Shrewsbury service. Dovey is virtually at sea level and can suffer badly from flooding. On 2nd January 1976, $\frac{1}{4}$ mile of embankment was washed away just to the south of the station in the vicinity of Glandyfi, and the route to Aberystwyth was closed until 14th April. Note the trackbed of the former non-platform Branch Loop (right) which had been removed the previous summer and the Main Loop (left), which has since been lifted.

Brought into use on 27th February 1959, Dovey Junction was the second of the final BR(WR) mechanical box design (Type 37). Built from 6ft long prefabricated panels, with vertical planking, this timber-framed cabin, to the standard 13ft width, housed a 65 lever, GW pattern, 5-bar vertical tappet frame. A solid canopy, hung from steel brackets, and a flat roof – a particularly poor design feature, especially at Welsh locations where there is more rainfall! – were provided. Both end panels had an operating floor door – this one behind the station nameplate being blanked off – to facilitate re-use elsewhere if required. Some 23 separate structures (affectionately and unofficially christened 'plywood wonders') have been identified, appearing at 32 different places; twelve are still in use.

Plate 197 (Opposite, bottom)
Class 59 No. 59001 *Yeoman Endeavour* comes off the Down Main at Westbury North Junction on 29th July 1987, with 6A09, the 09.05 Theale to Merehead Quarry empties. This is one of the many services supplying aggregates to the construction industry in the south east of England. The railway is the most cost effective method of moving aggregates over the distances involved but competition has caused Foster Yeoman to buy their own fleet of locomotives and build aluminium bodied wagons to increase the payload of their trains.

Fortunately PSB design in the 1980s has seen a welcome return to more traditional-looking buildings, instead of the somewhat sombre, austere carbuncular excesses of the previous two decades. With its panelled brickwork façade and splayed plinth foundation, and use of hipped roofs and bay windows, Westbury presents a functional, friendlier architectural approach – the BRB Director of Architecture, Design & Environment please note. Known by the signalmen as 'Colditz Castle' – notice the steel security fence – Westbury was opened on the weekend of 11-14th May 1984, after a five week closure of the station. It initially replaced the cabins at Westbury North, Heywood Road Junction, Fairwood Junction and Hawkeridge, and has since been extended in stages to take over the work of 16 mechanical boxes. The fringe boxes to Westbury are Exeter, Bristol, Reading and Salisbury PSBs, and Yeovil Pen Mill.

Plate 199
Opening on 6th November 1967, Dudley was the first Freightliner Terminal to be opened in the West Midlands. As traffic grew, the more centrally located Lawley Street was opened two years later, taking over services to Holyhead, Felixstowe, Harwich, London, Southampton and Tilbury. Freightliner commenced business late in 1965 – the original services operated to Glasgow, Newcastle and Stockton – but after a rapid expansion, rationalisations commenced as early as 1970, when the service connecting Par and Plymouth to Park Royal was discontinued due to a serious imbalance of traffic. The Dudley Terminal was closed in September 1986 and before April 1987, a further nine depots had disappeared. On 20th August 1985, Class 31/1 No. 31147 leaves the terminal with 4G53, the 18.30 service to Lawley Street.

For almost thirty years from 1954, the BR(LMR) Type 15 prefabricated design reigned supreme, with over 150 specimens. Roughly 35% were built of timber, with lapped boarding and small square locking room windows. A steel staircase led directly to the operating floor door, behind which was an interior porch and a second door into the operating room itself. This had a new window design, with a flat roof – actually it sloped slightly to the rear – and canopy with chamfered corners. Opened in 1967, with a 55 lever BR(LMR) standard frame, in connection with the Freightliner Terminal, Dudley worked AB to Eagle Crossing (left) and Round Oak South and closed in 1988.

Plate 200
The locomotive stabling sidings to the east of Manchester Victoria station are seen on 18th April 1981 with Class 08 No. 08676 and Class 40 No. 40047 as the sole occupants. Today, it is more likely to be a collection of Class 31s and 47s in a variety of liveries.

Since 1958, over 30 large PSBs have been built on the BR(LMR), all designed by the regional

Architect's staff. Various styles are apparent and Manchester Victoria East, arguably the ugliest, was constructed using a steel frame, with prefabricated concrete panels as a cladding material. On the ground floor, staff amenities facilities are provided, while the relay room is on the first floor and the control room on the top. Equipped with a Westinghouse 'OCS' panel and opened in 1962, Victoria East replaced six mechanical cabins. Originally prepared in 1955, the resignalling scheme had to be temporarily postponed because the Region's resources were being directed towards the completion of re-signalling between Manchester London Road/Liverpool and Crewe.

Plate 201
Prior to its demise on 1st May 1984, the Joint Goods line was used to allow freight traffic to avoid Carlisle station. Its premature end was caused by a runaway Freightliner train being diverted to prevent it running into Citadel station. The damage was never repaired. A service that would have used the former route is 9T07, the 16.55 Currock Carriage & Wagon Shops to Carlisle Yard trip, seen here approaching the station from the south on 6th February 1989. The train is made up of a selection of air-braked wagons: (TOPS code) 7 x VAA and 6 x VEA (vans), 1 x OAA (open wagon), 1 x HEA (hopper) and 4 x brakevans. Currock is the major wagon works for the Speedlink fleet.

Carlisle PSB, to the immediate right of the Class 08, was opened on 17th February 1973. Situated on the Down side, south of the station, it is one of six BR(LMR) examples built in the late 1960s and early 1970s, to a design which incorporated a brick faced lower storey, a control room with only a few small windows at each corner, and a large protruding sun canopy. Originally constructed with a flat roof, it was fitted with a new hipped roof about 1980 to provide improved protection from wet weather. Carlisle works TCB to fringe boxes at Annan, Motherwell PSB, Corby Gates, Howe & Co.'s Sidings, Preston PSB and Wigton. On 24th August 1986, the centre sidings between platforms 4 (left) and 3 were up-graded to bi-directionally signalled Goods Lines and new 3-aspect signals CE297 and CE296 replaced the former ground position lights.

Plate 202
On 26th August 1988, Class 47/0 No. 47231 *Silcock Express* passes through Upper Holloway with 7M52, the 15.11 Grays to Willesden Brent Sidings Speedlink service. It is composed exclusively of Polybulk wagons originating from the Tilbury Grain Terminal. The locomotive is in the two-tone grey livery adopted as standard by Railfreight in October 1987 to replace the original short-lived grey livery.

Since the middle 1980s, the BR(LMR) have chosen either large architect-designed structures or "Portakabins" as standard for all new boxes. Among the latter is Upper Holloway, which replaced its mechanical namesake on 10th Novem-

ber 1985. Erected on the Up side of the Tottenham & Hampstead line, adjacent to the Up Main to Up Reception Line connection, it also took over control of the former Junction Road Junction signal box area. Equipped with a small panel, it works TCB to Gospel Oak and West Hampstead PSB, and AB to Harringay Park Junction on the BR(ER).

Plate 203
Hauled by Class 20s Nos 20144 and 20156, the 6P62 Thrislington to Hartlepool Steetley service, composed of (TOPS code) PAA and PAB hoppers, passes slowly through Ferryhill Yard on 22nd March 1989. Off the photograph to the right, Class 37/3 No. 37378's train was being loaded at Thompson's Magnesium Limestone siding prior to being worked to Tyne Yard as part of the 6N13 trip. (Following the closure of Tyne Yard, this train, since 27th November 1989, has been diverted to Tees Yard.) An hour earlier, the 6S54 service had departed for the British Steel plant at Ravenscraig.

Ferryhill represents the BR(NER) development (mainly concerning the window details) of the LNER Type 13 design. When opened in 1952 (as Ferryhill No. 2 box) under a cabin amalgamation scheme, it was equipped with a 45 lever, McK&H, No. 17 pattern, 4in centres frame. Just discernible are the three square locking room windows, bricked up in 1971, when the frame was replaced by an IFS panel. This works to Darlington and Tyne Yard PSBs on the ECML (with CCTV supervision of Hett Mill level crossing); Whitwell box on the Leamside line, and Stillington (if switched out, Norton West), all of which are due to be closed on completion of the East Coast Electrification scheme.

Plate 204
On 22nd August 1987, Class 308/1 4-car emu No. 308147 approaches Broxbourne on the Up Main with the 14.34 Bishops Stortford to Liverpool Street service. Having arrived via the Up Passenger Loop, the 14.39 train from Hertford East was waiting at the adjacent platform, to provide a connection for local stations along the Lea Valley. Broxbourne was officially opened on 3rd November 1960, 100 yards north of the original station. At the same time extensive track modifications were carried out. These included the addition of the Down Passenger Loop and a coal concentration depot.

Situated on the Up side at the country end of the station, Broxbourne is one of 16 early BR(ER) modernisation panel boxes, built in the period 1958 – 1965 to Type 18. Most were required in connection with the electrification and resignalling of the former GE lines, although an isolated pocket of three examples are to be found as far north as the Sheffield area. All make extensive use of brick and concrete, and house a relay room and mess accommodation on the ground floor. The control room is largely glazed and provided with a 'sun baffle', which gives this design a most arresting appearance. Broxbourne was opened in 1960, with a Westinghouse 'N-X' panel, and its control area was extended on 31st January 1982 when Broxbourne Junction cabin was closed. TCB sections are to Cheshunt Junction, Roydon and St Margarets (on the Hertford East branch).

Plate 205

'Super Sprinter' Class 156 No. 156413 comes out of the Carriage Sidings at Colchester on 25th August 1988, to form the 15.14 departure for Birmingham New Street. Stabled on the right is Class 31/1 No. 31173 while to the left – partly eclipsed by the train – is the green-liveried Class 03 No. D2059 (03059) which had been withdrawn the previous year and was later acquired by the Isle of Wight Steam Railway. It was as a result of the 1962 Colchester Scheme that the diesel maintenance depot was constructed and the Down platform was converted to an island and extended to take 12-car trains. Also built at this time, though not illustrated, was a dive-under at the north end of the station for Down Clacton line services.

The seven large BR(ER) PSBs built since 1971 vary in style but all have a brick cladding. Sited near the London end of the Down platform 128 yards south of the 1962 power box which it initially replaced, Colchester PSB was opened on 4th December 1983. It has since been extended in stages to control a wide area of Suffolk, stretching from Marks Tey (in Essex) to Whitlingham Junction and Wymondham South, East Gate Junction and part of the Harwich Town branch.

Plate 206

Morning meeting at Gillingham (Dorset) on 28th August 1987, as Class 33/1 No. 33117 and Class 438/0 (Type 4-TC) No. 8030 'push/pull' set make up the 08.45 Sherborne to Waterloo train while Class 50 No. 50050 *Fearless* restarts the 07.00 Waterloo to Exeter St. Davids service. The Class 50s displaced Class 33s on the semi-fast trains to Exeter in 1980. After spending almost two decades under BR(WR) tutelage, Gillingham was transferred back to the BR(SR) in 1981.

Opened on 28th April 1957 to replace the original box on the opposite side of the line, Gillingham is one of several new boxes on the Salisbury–Exeter route, built to the BR(SR) Type 16 design. Rectangular in plan and constructed of brick, with a concrete canopy and flat roof, the cabin has no locking room windows. The steel-framed operating floor windows have a short fixed section at the head, with a brick pillar at the centre front. In its comparatively short life, Gillingham has seen a number of developments: the singling of the line in 1967; and the replacement by colour lights of the semaphore signals. However, the cabin still retains its 30 lever, Westinghouse A3 frame.

Plate 207
Class 101 dmus have been regularly seen on the BR(SR) since Old Oak Common was made responsible for operating the Tonbridge-
-Redhill–Reading route. Making a dirty departure from Guildford on 28th August 1988, set L839 (cars 53310, 59526 and 53326)
forms the 09.28 (SuO) Gatwick Airport to Reading service. Guildford station was in the process of being demolished prior to a
£6 million rebuilding programme which was completed at the end of 1989.

**Opened on 17th April 1966, Guildford was the first of six BR(SR) Type 19 boxes, built to the 'Clasp' system of pre-fabricated concrete
panels. It replaced twelve existing mechanical cabins, among them Guildford Yard, dating back to 1878, whose signal box letter code
WX was transferred to the new PSB. Situated at the London end of the station, on the Up side, Guildford has an 'N-X' control panel,
supervising an area bounded by Ash Crossing, Woking, Surbiton PSB, Wimbledon PSB, Shalford and Farncombe boxes. Note the illuminated position 1, junction indicator above WX14 signal.**

Plate 208
The passenger services between
Edinburgh Waverley and Airdrie
were withdrawn on 9th January
1956 but the former North British line via Plains remained
open as a through route for
freight services until early in
1982. Today, Bathgate is the
eastern and Drumgelloch the
western terminus. When this
photograph was taken on 14th
April 1987, Airdrie was the end
of the line for all traffic since
freight traffic to Inverhouse
ceased in August 1985. Arriving
on the former Down line at
Airdrie – since used for the
extension to Drumgelloch –
Class 311 emu No. 311092 forms
the 10.54 from Helensburgh.

**Airdrie cabin was built in connection with the Glasgow Suburban Electrification scheme, Stage 1 of which was inaugurated in November
1960 by Sir Brian Robertson, the then chairman of the BTC. Though very similar in design to the contemporaneous examples on the
BR(ER) and BR(NER), the signal box, a BR(ScR) Type 16c, has a deeper concrete surround to the first floor windows. Situated on
the now disused Up platform, Airdrie contains a 30 lever, Stevens pattern lever frame, working the points, shunt signals and formerly
the detonator placers mechanically, but the running signals are worked electrically by individual thumb switches. This hybrid method
– part mechanical, part electrical – has been used since the 1930s for comparative cheapness. Yoker IECC, scheduled for completion
in 1990, will control all lines from Helensburgh to Airdrie, plus the branches to Milngavie, Springburn and Balloch.**

Plate 209
On 7th May 1988, Class 37/4 No. 37414 stands at Inverness' platform 6 with the stock forming the 18.15 (SO) to Kyle of Lochalsh. These ETH locomotives were converted from Class 37/0s at Crewe Works in 1985 and 1986. The first were delivered to ScotRail at the end of June 1985 and their debut on the Kyle line was in January 1986. No. 37414 was released from Crewe Works in October 1985 and after being used for crew training at Crewe Diesel Depot, it proceeded to Scotland. It spent a short time at Eastfield TMD before being despatched to Inverness in January 1986.

Inverness Signalling Centre – a grandiose title for a most unprepossessing building – is symptomatic of the general malaise affecting architectural design on BR today (the BRB Director of Architecture, Design & Environment please note again!), and shows another of the many contrasting styles of signal box architecture found in the 1980s. Photographed from platform 6 and sandwiched between platforms 5 (for northbound trains), where the locomotive is standing, and 4 (for southbound departures), with the Repair Shops behind, Inverness is the first deployment of a large SSI – the pilot scheme at Leamington Spa was fully commissioned in September 1985, and has operated very reliably since. Opened on 7th March 1987, it replaced five mechanical cabins in the immediate area and worked as a first stage to fringe boxes at Clachnaharry, Aviemore and Nairn. In October 1988, it became the RETB Communications Centre for the Far North and Kyle lines, superseding the original RETB installation at Dingwall.

14 : Aberdeen Before Resignalling

Plate 210
Over the years, in the short distance (less than two miles) between Aberdeen North and Craiginches South cabins, there have been at least 13 different boxes. The GNoS Aberdeen North box was opened on 16th August 1914, replacing its predecessor of the same name which stood immediately to the south (right), at the end of the then No. 6 platform. It contained a 150 lever, Stevens frame until 1970, when track rationalisation associated with the singling of the former GNoS main line necessitated its replacement by a new 20 lever frame. On 26th July 1981, Aberdeen North was closed and its area was controlled from Aberdeen PSB.

Plate 211
Situated on the centre of Nos 7 and 8 platforms, Aberdeen Centre box was opened on 4th October 1914 as a replacement for Aberdeen Joint Station box and a temporary cabin, Aberdeen West. Equipped with a 60 lever, Caledonian (Stevens pattern) frame, it was of necessity a narrow building giving the signalmen the minimum of operating space. The cabin's main function was to control the scissors crossovers between Nos 6 and 7 and Nos 8 and 9 platforms (see Plate 217). Three of these four through lines (platforms Nos 6, 7 and 8) between North, Centre and South boxes were bi-directional and worked under Permissive Block regulations (No. 9 platform was worked in the Down direction only).

Plate 212
Class 47/4 No. 47517 (since named *Andrew Carnegie*) leaves the "Granite City" with the 14.40 departure for Edinburgh on 14th August 1980. With the exception of the ECML HST services all other passenger trains are now worked by Class 156/158 'Sprinters'.

A view from Aberdeen South box of the trackwork and signalling at the south end of the station. The gantry supported no fewer than 17 signal arms on eight dolls, with calling-on signals and stencil route indicators below the main signals. The two miniature arm signals above the locomotive were for shunting from the North British and Caledonian Yards, while the tubular steel bracket on the extreme right controlled the exit from the Great North Yard. Notice the enormous rodding run leading to and beyond the lattice bracket on the left, which governed entry to Nos 9 (nearest camera) and 8 platforms. No. 138 signal was cleared for the train to leave from No. 4 bay platform.

Plate 213
On 14th August 1980, preparation for an evening sleeper departure begins in the mid-afternoon as Class 08 No. 08855 pushes the stock past Clayhills carriage and HST inspection shed. Since November 1987, when the diesel depot at Ferryhill closed, locomotives are stabled near this facility.

Of Aberdeen South's three signal gantries, this was the most southern. In 1947, when the new signalling was commissioned, it had a total of thirteen arms, controlling the entry and exit from the Carriage Sidings and Loop Line (on the left), the Down and Up West Lines, and the Down and Up Main Lines (extreme right). The shunter on the Up West Line was propelling stock back into the station under the authority of No. 22 shunt signal (out of sight behind the vehicles).

Plate 214
Coming off the ¾ mile viaduct which extends from the station to Ferryhill, Class 40 No. 40073 makes an impressive start as it heads the 13.40 departure for Glasgow on 25th August 1981. In 1967, the former Caledonian Railway Buchanan Street station was closed and the line between Stanley and Kinnaber Junctions ceased to be a through route. Since then, these trains have been diverted via Dundee and terminate at the ex-NB Glasgow Queen Street station.

Viewed looking towards the station, this gantry was the middle of three controlled by Ferryhill Junction box, 656 yards south of Aberdeen South. Between these, the old Denburn South Junction and Clayhills Sidings cabins were situated. The gantry controlled movements only on the three right-hand lines – the Up and Down Main, and the Goods Line. Four of the eleven dolls have had their signal arms removed, and on either side of No. 61 Up Main Line Home signal (at clear) can be seen the remains of No. 84 Up Main to Engine Sheds (left) and No. 87 Up Goods to Engine Sheds (right). The doll third from the left carried No. 55 Down Main Starter with Aberdeen South's distant below.

Plate 215
Class 08 No. 08855 moves twelve Mark I vehicles past Ferryhill on 14th August 1980. For four months Ferryhill was the temporary terminus of what was to become the CR main line. It was not until 2nd August 1854 that the railway reached the more centrally located Guild Street station (now the Goods depot). At one stage, the financial position was so poor that the railway company considered a terminus south of the River Dee! From November 1867, all passenger services were concentrated at the Joint station.

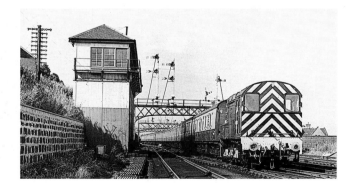

Ferryhill Junction, the second box to bear this name, was opened with a 104 lever frame in 1908, when the West Lines, adjacent to the cabin, were inaugurated. Architecturally, it was unusual for two reasons: normally wooden boxes were not found north of the Central Lowlands, and it had been painted in the former GNoS colours for this type of building: green (lower part) and yellow (upper). At one time, it controlled the junction of the Deeside branch to Ballater, which diverged behind and to the left of the photographer. The Class 08 was shunting under the authority of No. 21 Up West Line to Engine Sheds signal. On the extreme left, next to No. 5 Down West Line Starter (with Aberdeen South distant below) was No. 43 Down West to Down Main Line Home and distant.

Plate 216
Class 47/4 No. 47464 nears journey's end on 25th August 1981, as it passes Craiginches with the 11.35 service from Glasgow Queen Street. Craiginches Yard was an important focus for Speedlink traffic before it was transferred to the Guild Street Goods Depot in July 1988. After failing at Elgin on 23rd September 1986, while hauling the 09.35 Aberdeen to Inverness train, the locomotive came to a premature end: it sustained extensive front-end damage when the rescuing engine, Class 37/4 No. 37416, commandeered from an Up service, failed to stop!

Craiginches North box, 935 yards south of Ferryhill Junction, controlled the entrance to the Up side of Craiginches Yard (left), and the exit from the Down Yard Departure Siding (right). It was a typical Caledonian Railway brick box, extremely tall, since a road overbridge (from which this photograph was taken), came between it and the yard. Working AB to Ferryhill and Craiginches South, it had a 30 lever Stevens frame, only one of which (No. 30) was spare, until the declining use of the Up Yard made track simplification inevitable. 115 yards south of North box was No. 19 Up Main Starter (with Craiginches South No. 12 distant below) and No. 6 Up Main to Centre Sidings bracketed off left, while No. 24 Down Main Home showed all clear.

Plate 217
Situated 88 yards north of Aberdeen Centre, these lattice post signals, underslung from the station canopy, were the No. 9 platform signals protecting the crossover between it and No. 8 platform. No. 30 (left) was the Up Home to No. 8 platform, while No. 25 (below) was the "cat's eyes", displaying a Warning (W) or Calling-on (C) in the stencil route indicator, to No. 8 platform occupied. No. 17 (miniature arm) read to the Carriage Sidings or Clayhills Loop. Note the counterbalance weights and signal wires above the arms, both of which were shorter than normal to avoid fouling the structure gauge.

Plate 218
To mark the demise of the Class 55s, BR organised eleven "Deltic Farewell" excursions between 17th October 1981 and 2nd January 1982. The advertising stated "... tours to mark the end of an era...". The various 'Deltics' selected penetrated every Region and reached such disparate locations as Exeter, Bournemouth and Lowestoft. One of the two excursions which started from Newcastle went to Aberdeen on 17th October 1981. On the outward leg, No. 55009 *Ballymoss* worked as far as Perth, where Class 27s Nos 27037 and 27029 took the train to Inverness. For the section to Aberdeen, Class 40 No. 40167 was substituted. *Ballymoss* reflects the last of the day's autumn sunlight as it prepares to leave on the return run.

The dismembered remains of semaphore signals from the south end of No. 7 platform were awaiting removal two months after Aberdeen Centre and South cabins had been closed on 9th August 1981. The scheme to simplify the station layout and introduce MAS cost £3 million. The "Granite City" and its environs is now signalled from a PSB, opened on 21st June 1981 and situated 500 yards south of the station on the Down (west) side. By today's standards, its control area is quite small. It links up with Newtonhill box some ten miles to the south, working TCB on the Down Main, and AB on the Up; and with Dyce (formerly South) cabin on the single line 6½ miles to the north.

15 : Gantries

Plate 219

An unofficial livery first seen in 1978, and particularly associated with Finsbury Park diesel depot, was a white stripe applied to the bodyside of some Class 31 locomotives. Part of the line is still visible, above the number of Class 31/4 No. 31411 as it passes Falsgrave signal box on 26th May 1984, with the 13.25 York to Scarborough service. This train was part of a diagram which involved three return journeys between York and the resort.

Regrettably, only one of the many gantries which used to grace the approaches to Scarborough survives today. Erected in 1908 in connection with the new Falsgrave box (right), this fine McK&H specimen used to carry 15 arms and since 25th November 1984, presides over a slim-line station layout. The two dolls on the left govern access to and egress from the three Up Sidings, while No. 17 (tallest arm, left) and No. 57 below apply to the Up Main (centre line). All the other signals refer to the bi-directional Down Main on which trains may leave and approach the station (though hopefully not at the same time!). When the photograph was taken, four levers worked the theatre route indicator – No. 67 for the calling-on arm and Nos 69 (for "C" Road), 70 and 71 for the main arm. Note the old lever numbers (99, 101, 105 and 109) near the top of the wooden doll, and the famous No. 1A bay platform (right), $\frac{1}{4}$ mile from the ticket barrier, whence Whitby trains used to depart.

Plate 220

On 31st May 1984, the 6E91 Moss Sidings to Haverton Hill Exchange Sidings service arrives over one hour early and stands on the Up Goods Loop at Skipton while awaiting the relief crew. The train is headed by Class 31/1s Nos 31200 and 31215 and composed of empty short wheel base anhydrous ammonia tanks complete with barrier vehicles. This daily working was inaugurated in 1977 when the ammonia plant at ICI Heysham was closed. The continued run-down resulted in the train running on MThFO from January 1985 until the complete closure of the works in 1986.

Of all the regions, the BR(LMR) has the greatest number of signal gantries still in use. This one at Skipton Station North Junction spans the Down Main towards Hellifield (left), the Up Main and the Up Goods Loop, on which the train is waiting. It protects the crossovers between it and the box (off the picture to the right) and also the double junction, which amalgamates to form the single line Swinden Quarry branch. In the late 1970s, this was worked by "No Signalman" Token Block regulations – a system similar to EKT working, but where the train crews themselves instead of the signalmen issue and return the tokens to the machines, which are located at each end of the section in buildings other than signal cabins. Below No. 29 Up Main Home is Skipton Station South Junction's motor-worked distant; to their right is No. 40 Up Main to Branch. The Up Goods Loop miniature arm reads three ways: No. 9 (stencil S) to the Up Sidings; No. 47 (stencil M) to the Up Main; and No. 48 (stencil B) to the branch.

Plate 221
Class 40 No. 40034 roars out of Rhyl on 6th August 1983 with the 09.25 (SO) Llandudno to Euston train. (The locomotive was deputising for a Crewe allocated Class 47/4. It continued the diagram by returning from Crewe with the 09.55 (SO) Euston to Holyhead service.) This vintage machine was named *Accra* in May 1962. Unfortunately the name was removed in the early 1970s but the fixing bolts are still conspicuous on the bodyside.

Based on the LNW design, perpetuated by the LMS, with wooden dolls and the usual double hand-rail, the gantry at Rhyl No. 1 signal box shows signs of an even more glorious past. Spanning what was once a quadruple track section of line, and situated at the London end of the station, it authorises movements on the Down Slow (left foreground) to the Down Passenger line (No. 12 signal, left) and the Down Platform line (No. 8, taller arm), and on the Down Fast (centre road) to the Down Passenger (No. 5 signal, centre doll), the Down Platform (No. 4), and the Down Through line (No. 2, right). The distant arms belong to Rhyl No. 2 cabin.

Plate 222 (Opposite, top)
In its long career, the "North Country Continental" boat train has visited all the main Manchester stations with the exception of the former Exchange. The train was inaugurated in 1885, and until September 1963, it connected Harwich with Liverpool Central. For the next twenty years, Piccadilly became the northerly terminus until the service was extended to Glasgow via Victoria. The view shows the 07.17 Harwich to Glasgow Central "European" service on 13th August 1983, headed by Class 47/4 No. 47590, as it approaches Collyhurst Street. In 1988, the Provincial Sector replaced the loco-hauled formation with a 'Super Sprinter' which called at Piccadilly and Oxford Road, before continuing to Blackpool.

To our knowledge, there are now no semaphore gantries on the BR(AR), so here is a third example from the BR(LMR), this time at Miles Platting Station Junction (the cabin is behind the fourth coach). It is of the later LMS design, with tubular steel dolls and a single hand-rail, and was built across six lines to carry the Down Fast (arms removed from left-hand dolls), the Down Slow and the Down East Goods Home signals. The train is weaving from the Up Main (from Philip's Park No. 1 box) to the Up Fast (second line from the left) on the 1 in 49 descent past Collyhurst Street cabin to Manchester Victoria station.

Plate 223 (Opposite, bottom)
On 24th August 1981, having just undergone an intermediate overhaul at St Rollox works, Class 26 No. 26035 combines – for 'running-in' purposes – with Class 27/0 No. 27010, to head the 13.39 Dundee to Glasgow Queen Street service into Dunblane, past the former junction with the Oban line. Since November 1965, Oban services have been diverted to the West Highland route, and stations such as Callander, Bahquidder and Killin Junction disappeared from the railway map.

Situated 95 yards south of the signal box just visible above the first coach, this neat lattice Caledonian gantry at the north end of Dunblane station used to carry four signals. Reading from left to right, No. 41 signal was the Down Platform Loop Home to the former Callander branch, while No. 42 applied to the Down Main towards Perth. No. 43 was the Down Main (centre foreground) to Callander Branch Home signal and No. 45 is the Down Main Second Home. Note all the ball and spike finials remain intact.

Plate 224
At its zenith, High Wycombe boasted expresses into two London termini. Between Ashendon and Northolt Junctions, the GC services out of Marylebone shared the route with the GW out of Paddington. Even though the services have been drastically 'pruned' over the past couple of decades, the basic infrastructure still remained intact when this photograph was taken on Good Friday 1984. Class 115 dmu (cars 51652, 59653, 59650 and 51880) leave the station with the 09.50 Banbury to Marylebone train.

Although there are still many semaphores on posts and brackets on the BR(WR), gantries are now a rarity. South of the station at High Wycombe, once the junction for the Maidenhead line via Bourne End, is a small example, consisting of little more than an extended bracket supported by a retaining wall, and spanning the Up Platform and Up Main lines. Two 4ft high dolls, carrying the Up Main and Up Platform to Maidenhead line signals, formerly on either side of the 9ft tall Up Main signal, have been removed. The arms are all 4ft long, centre-balance signals, and a description and fully dimensioned drawing of this gantry appears in *GWS*, page 44.

16 : Shrewsbury – A Case Study in Semaphores

Plate 225

This splendid panorama from Severn Bridge Junction signal box shows the castle (far left) and the prison (far right) and how part of the station was extended over the River Severn by the construction of a new girder bridge in 1902. The openness of the station is noticeable, but this was not always the case. A substantial footbridge was removed in 1961 and the last of the overall roof was demolished in 1963. These changes facilitated the setting back of the southern part of platform 3 to provide three lines throughout the length of the station between platforms 3 and 4. Today, however, platform 3 sees little traffic; since 1969, all passenger traffic has been concentrated on the island platform. Reference to Plate 228 shows the Class 08 to be stabled in Siding 1 (former platform 1) with a rake of Departmental (TOPS code) ZHV wagons loaded with spent ballast – note the holes in the wagon sides to prevent overloading. Class 37/4 No. 37428 is leaving bay platform 5, via No. 82 points, with the 10.48 service for Aberystwyth, while the Class 101 dmu is forming the delayed 10.43 service for Llandovery from bay platform 6. With the exception of Plate 230, all photographs in this chapter were taken on 10th August 1988.

With the widespread introduction of block working in the 1880s, it was important for the signalman to have a good view of the lines he controlled, particularly at busy junctions and stations, since in those days, there was no track circuiting to help the signalman to identify a train's precise position. Severn Bridge is staffed continuously by two signalmen, except on Sundays when only one man is on duty. To the north, it works to Crewe Junction box (Plate 231), although until the early 1960s, an intermediate cabin, called Central, with 69 levers, stood at the buffer-stops of the present bay platforms 5 and 6.

Plate 226
Class 150/1 'Sprinter' No. 150104 approaches Severn Bridge Junction forming the 09.15 local service from Wolverhampton. On the right are the station avoiding lines, for many years used only by freight trains, such as the South Wales to Albion Gulf Oil. Formerly the last regular passenger service to use this route was the summer Saturdays "Cambrian Coast Express", which was discontinued in 1967. An interesting development in the 1989 Summer timetable was the scheduling of the 09.40(SO) Pwllheli to Euston train via the Up Loop, allowing a non-stop run between Welshpool and Wellington.

For 70 years from 1862, Shrewsbury came under the joint control of the LNW and GW, with a Joint Superintendent in charge. GW semaphores predominate in this view from Severn Bridge towards Abbey Foregate box (just visible to the right of the gantry in the distance), on the approach from Wolverhampton, a joint line signalled by the GW. The 'Sprinter' has just passed No. 74 Down Bays to Platform 5 signal. The Up and Down Loop lines on the extreme right, forming an independent route avoiding the station itself, join the Up and Down Hereford lines at English Bridge Junction, where there was once a signal box. This junction (points 174 and 175) is now controlled from Severn Bridge box, which with four other neighbouring cabins, is scheduled to be replaced by a small SSI installation in the station buildings in the autumn of 1991.

Plate 227
The highly polished operating floor of Severn Bridge Junction box, with its 180 lever LNW tumbler frame – now the largest mechanical frame in Britain – creates an atmosphere of purposeful business. Most of the levers are back or "normal" in the frame, but about ten have been pulled "reverse". In this particular pattern of frame, the catch handles (mechanical devices to keep the levers fully in the normal or reverse position in the frame) are on the front of the levers, and resemble stirrups. They activate the mechanical interlocking as they are depressed before pulling or pushing a lever. Levers are painted in almost every colour according to their particular function and various colour combinations are also used: for example lever 13 in the immediate foreground is red with a white horizontal band halfway down to denote a starting (or section) signal electrically released from the normal position by the block instrument of the box in advance (in this case Abbey Foregate) being placed to the Line Clear position. The various block instruments themselves, block bells, telephones, signal repeaters and other accessories are mounted on the block (or instrument) shelf above the frame. At the far end is one of the track diagrams.

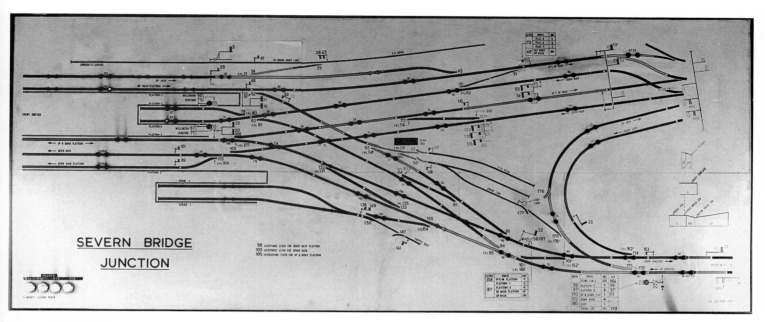

Plate 228
Every signal box has a track diagram on which appears a plan layout (not to scale) of all the points and signals controlled from the cabin. Usually, it would be suspended from the roof above the block shelf, but because of the restricted height of the operating floor, Severn Bridge in fact has two, one at each end of the lever frame. With the general introduction of track circuiting early this century, illuminated track diagrams have been provided. Nowadays, red lights on the diagram itself are lit when a train occupies a section of line. In this view, the 09.15 terminating dmu from Crewe is in Up Main platform 7, while the 'Sprinter' seen in Plate 226 is about to form the 10.10 departure for Birmingham New Street from platform 5.

Plate 229
Although transferred to the BR(LMR) on 1st January 1963, Abbey Foregate proudly displays its GW origins nearly 30 years later. Standing beneath the gantry, our guide on this occasion, Len Lord, the Relief Traffic Manager, acknowledges the driver of Class 47/4 No. 47584 *County of Suffolk,* heading the 11.04 departure for Euston. Before the full electrified service between Euston and Wolverhampton was implemented in May 1967, trains for London were routed via Birmingham Snow Hill and terminated at Paddington.

Extensive improvements during 1914, including a dock opposite Abbey Foregate box to deal with traffic for the Royal Show, and the opening of the Loop lines, meant the construction of two new cabins at English Bridge junction and Abbey Foregate. A GW Type 7 design, the box contains a 93 lever frame. It works AB to Severn Bridge on the four lines to the station, and on the Up and Down Loops; and, since 27th January 1985, to Wellington. The locomotive has just passed No. 7 Up Main Starting signal. On the left of the gantry are the Down Main Home signals: No. 84 (plus Severn Bridge fixed distant below) to the Down Loop line; No. 90 (and Severn Bridge fixed distant) to the Down Main; and No. 89 to the Down Bays line (ultimately leading to platforms 5 and 6). The gantry's poor physical condition led to its demolition later in 1988.

Plate 230
On 21st August 1985, Class 25/2 No. 25201 prepares to take the Cambrian line at Sutton Bridge with the 7T70 Coton Hill to Welsh-pool trip. The open wagons (TOPS code) OBA were loaded with timber for Welshpool and the two wagons of rails were for Hookagate. (Both facilities have since been closed.) The line in the foreground lead to Kidderminster via the Severn Valley. When the last section of the Shropshire & Montgomeryshire Railway closed in 1960, the BR(WR) built a short curve to connect the Severn Valley route to the Abbey Foregate Esso terminal. Latterly, until the depot's closure in July 1988, this was the only use made of the branch. The large area of open space to the right was the site of the GW and LNW locomotive sheds.

From the footbridge adjacent to Sutton Bridge box looking towards Shrewsbury, the sharp curvature of the line past the Abbey and Severn Bridge cabin on the extreme left is apparent. The train is leaving the Loco Siding via No. 44 points under the authority of ground disc signal No. 47, hidden by the location box at the foot of the bracket signal. No. 49 (miniature arm) signal reads to the Down Goods Running Loop; No. 58 (centre) is the Down Main Home towards Dorrington box, while No. 54 signal applies Down Main Home to Welshpool single line. Since the commissioning of the Cambrian line RETB scheme in October 1988, Sutton Bridge has worked directly to the one surviving box at Machynlleth, nerve-centre of the new system. Here, two signalmen's work stations, (the other one covering the lines to Aberystwyth and Pwllheli), complete with VDU track displays and radio communications equipment, are positioned beside the mechanical lever frame that is still needed to operate the conventional signalling in the station area and the TCB section to Dovey Junction.

Plate 232
As a result of track rationalisation in the station, the Up Goods Loop (left) at Shrewsbury Crewe Bank is frequently used to allow heavy freight trains – especially those working via the Down Hereford line – to be overtaken. An instruction, which emanated from the Area Manager's Office in 1988, required 6V75, the 06.35 Mossend to Cardiff Tidal Sidings steel coil train to be held on this line to allow the 13.17 Liverpool Lime Street to Cardiff service to proceed. Making a vigorous start out of the station, Class 37/4 No. 37430 *Cwmbran* leads the 14.00 Cardiff Central to Manchester Piccadilly train.

As its name suggests, Crewe Bank is at the foot of the 1 in 124 climb to Crewe, 32 miles away. Situated on the Down side 579 yards from Crewe Junction, it was built about 1943 to ARP specifications for World War II. Designated LMS Type 13, all had flat roofs and made extensive use of concrete and brick, but of the Big Four companies, only the LMS relieved the austerity somewhat by featuring a blue brick base, and two bands (generally of three courses each) of blue bricks near the operating floor level. Like most ARP boxes, the frame is at the back and now only 13 of the 45 levers are in use. Photographed from the Up Goods Loop, where steam specials are watered by the fire brigade from the adjacent fire station (off left), the box is a Class B, one- man job, working 09.00 to 17.00 and is closed at other times except for special engineering work on Sundays.

Plate 231 (Opposite, bottom)
Having previously been stabled on the Down Platform Loop (platform 3), Class 150/1 No. 150103 reverses into the station to form the 14.44 departure for Crewe (via Chester). The modern office block, much of which is eclipsed by the Post Office conveyor, was the area's main BR administrative block until the original station building was renovated.

Crewe Junction box, a LNW Type 4 design of 1903, containing a 120 lever LNW tumbler frame, controls the junction of the two routes to Crewe (off the left of the picture) and Chester, working AB to Crewe Bank and Baschurch cabins respectively. Its height is deceptive, as it is constructed on an embankment and the back is built up from street level. The locking room windows have all been bricked up and a new fire exit has been added. A number of piecemeal alterations to the track layout and signalling have taken place over the years, culminating in the removal of the fine gantry spanning the Crewe lines and the replacement by colour lights of some semaphores on the gantry at the north end of the station earlier in 1988. The left-hand arms of the bracket signal read from the Chester direction to the Up Main, avoiding the station platforms, while the principal route is to Up Main Platform 7. The 'Sprinter' is about to pass No. 3 signal into Up & Down Platform 4, the only through platform signalled for reversible working.

17 : A Decade of Change

Plate 233
Deputising for a March based Class 31, Class 25/1 No. 25035 leaves Norwich on 30th May 1981 with the 12.52(SO) Yarmouth to Peterborough train. This was the first year that no passenger services were scheduled to use the short, 617 yards Wensum Curve, linking Trowse Swing Bridge with Wensum Junction. Allowing through trains to/from Yarmouth to avoid a reversal at Norwich, this line was used in the final years by only three Up and three Down Saturday seasonal services. The last was the 10.50(SO) Yarmouth to Liverpool Street, which ceased on 20th September 1980. However, in 1986, it was temporarily re-instated as a normal running line to help overcome the problems resulting from the shutdown of the main station, when most services terminated at Trowse.

A glorious hotchpotch of semaphore signals and one colour light existed at the approach to Norwich station in the late 1970s. On the extreme left was a 4-way shunting signal, while above the rear cab of the Class 25 was another shunting signal with a six-way stencil route indicator. On the bracket signal, No. 40 Up Main Home (slotted with Trowse Swing Bridge box) was at clear, while No. 38 (miniature arm reading to the Up Goods) and No. 39 (top arm, slotted with Wensum Junction box) and No. 33 (shunt-ahead) applied to the Down Branch to Wensum Junction. Immediately to the right of the Up Main was the Wensum Loop line, which afforded a route from Norwich to Wensum Junction completely independent of the Up Main. In the left foreground were the Arrival and Departure lines to and from the Goods Station, which had its own signal box.

Plate 234
The first electric train to reach Norwich arrived on 6th April 1987, followed three days later by the first passenger service, a special staff excursion from Liverpool Street. The full InterCity service commenced on 12th May. After the transformation resulting from electrification and resignalling, Class 47/3 No. 47341 and Class 47/4 No. 47472 are leaving the Freight Depot two hours early, on 30th August 1988, with the 6H90 Speedlink for Whitemoor. Class 86/2 No. 86216 *Meteor* had arrived with the 10.30 service from Liverpool Street and had been released to the headshunt after the 13.00 departure. The next train for London is waiting in platform 2.

Today, hardly a signal in sight, but plenty of OLE instead. In the intervening years between these pictures, the signalling at Norwich was transformed in a number of stages. On the weekend of 1st-2nd February 1986, Norwich Passenger Yard box was closed and its area controlled from a new Norwich Station Temporary box. This was itself taken out of use and replaced by the new Norwich Station panel box on 8th June 1986, with AB working being retained to Norwich Thorpe Junction box (behind the photographer). It closed on 13th July 1986, when its area was worked from Norwich box with TCB being instituted to Trowse Swing Bridge and Whitlingham Junction cabins. On the weekend of 29- 30th November 1986 Norwich panel was extended to include Trowse Lower Junction and Trowse Yard cabins, which were closed, TCB being worked to Colchester PSB and Hethersett. Trowse Swing Bridge was reduced to a bridge control box. The final stage came on 15th March 1987 when Norwich panel box itself ceased to operate and Colchester PSB took over control.

Plate 235
This view of Chaloners Whin in August 1983 depicts an important junction. Here, the 09.00 King's Cross to Edinburgh service takes the Down Doncaster line while the Stanier "Black 5" No. 5305, heading the 08.35 ex-York "Scarborough Spa Express", prepares to cross over from the Down Normanton to the Down Leeds line. Running three times a week, from mid-July until the end of August, this train took the circular route from York to Leeds via Harrogate, proceeding thence to Scarborough. After the lifting of the 'steam ban', the first steam-hauled special train over the York to Scarborough line was hauled by A4 Pacific No. 19 *Bittern* on 16th September 1972. Regular steam hauled trains returned in June 1978.

Sanctioned in 1937 and due for completion in 1942, the previous major resignalling of York was finally brought into use in April 1951, due to the intervention of World War II. By today's standards of modern power signalling, it was a comparatively small scheme, involving the closure of seven cabins, among them Locomotive Yard, with the longest mechanical frame (295 levers) in the world, and, to the south, Chaloners Whin box (formerly on the site of the nameboard). Here, the new NE main line cut-off to Selby, opened in 1871, swung off to the left, while the quadruple track section, dating from the widening of the line in 1904, to Normanton (centre pair of lines), and Leeds (right) joined in a series of double junctions. The layout is so arranged that the trains are about to miss each other!

Plate 236
The second view was taken six years later on 28th March 1989 and, to avoid the catenary, about ten metres to the east. Passing the former junction on the Down Leeds line, Class 37/5s Nos 37507 *Hartlepool Pipe Mill* and 37509 head 6E40, the 10.07 Corby to Lackenby service, composed of (TOPS code) BBA empty coil wagons.

Before the intrusion of the 25kV OLE, the scene at Chaloners Whin Junction was transformed by the effects of the Selby Coalfield, necessitating the construction of a new section of the ECML, between Temple Hirst and Colton Junctions, which began in February 1980, and the abandonment, from 3rd October 1983, of the 1871 line (now filled in, left, and further south, part of a walkway). More recently, the junctions were removed and resited in connection with the latest MAS programme at York, whose IECC, replacing what was at the time in 1951 the largest Westinghouse 'OCS' relay interlocking in the world, with 825 routes, is the first to be commissioned on the BR(ER). Housed in a comparatively small building west of the station, it will ultimately control an area bounded by fringe boxes at Poppleton, Gateshead (called Tyneside), Bowesfield, Strensall, Selby, Doncaster and Church Fenton.

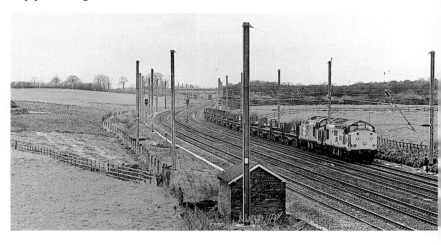

Plate 237
Six years also separate these photographs of Chester East Junction. On 13th August 1982, Class 40 No. 40092 bypasses the station on the Up Goods line and prepares to take the Down Warrington line with 6F27, the 10.13 Penmaenmawr to St Helens loaded ballast train.

Now you see it: commanding a good view of the eastern end of the station and situated between platform 4 and 5 lines, Chester No. 2 box was a magnificent three-storey structure to LNW Type 5, measuring 96ft 6in by 12ft (size U). With a 182 lever LNW frame at the back, it used to work Permissive Block to Chester No. 1 box, the junction of the Warrington and Crewe lines, 200 yards away (to the right). Towards the station it also worked PB to No. 3 on the Down Main and Down Platform lines (extreme left), and PB to No. 3A cabin on the remaining lines. Note the fire escape ladder – a requirement of the Health & Safety at Work Act.

Plate 238
The more recent view taken on 19th August 1988, shows a Class 108 dmu (cars 54251 and 53968) with the 11.28 Chester to Manchester Oxford Road local service via the ex-CLC route. It is leaving platform 6, one of the eastern end bays of the "new centre platform", brought into use in 1890. Prior to this, all through traffic was concentrated on the present platform 3A/B, by means of a scissors crossing enabling Up and Down trains to pass. Platform renumbering in connection with further remodelling took place on 5th October 1980.

Now you don't: weed-infested ballast below the dmu marks the site of Chester No. 2 box. It was closed on 6th May 1984, two days after the commissioning of Chester PSB. Situated adjacent to the Down Warrington line, to the right of this photograph the PSB contains a 'N-X' panel, working as a first stage, TCB to fringe cabins at Green Lane, Mold Junction, Hooton, Mickle Trafford and Beeston Castle – a fairly small area of 55 single track miles. However, as finance permits, future extensions to Ruabon, Prestatyn, Warrington PSB (via Hooton and Helsby), Plumley and Crewe PSB (via Sandbach and Beeston Castle) are envisaged.

Plate 239
Yet again six years separate the two views at Welsh's Bridge. On 26th June 1982, Class 27/1 No. 27108 approaches Inverness station with the 11.50 service from Aberdeen. When new in July 1962, as No. D5396, it was delivered to Cricklewood (Depot code 14A). Besides those members of the class allocated to the BR(ScR), the other BRC&W Co. Bo-Bo Class 2s were based in the BR(NER) at Thornaby (51L) and the BR(ER) at Hornsey (34B). It was not until early 1971 that all Class 26/27s were concentrated in Scotland.

The eastern entrance to Inverness station was characterised in semaphore days by two gantries at Welsh's Bridge box. This, the outer one, spanned the Forres Lines, and carried the Down Home and shunting signals for both the Forres and Aviemore Lines. It was taken out of use on 14th February 1987 when Welsh's Bridge was closed and the Aviemore Lines were singled between Rose Street cabin and Milburn Junction (far distance, right).

Plate 240
When this photograph was taken on 7th May 1988, the Class 27s had been displaced by Class 47/4s. The new order, represented by No. 47541 *The Queen Mother,* painted in the ScotRail livery introduced in 1984, is heading the 13.40 train from Aberdeen. Diesel locomotives have been responsible for services on this route for only a short time. In March 1980, Class 27s took over from the dmus which had worked the line since steam was displaced in 1959.

This picture shows the dramatic changes brought about by the introduction of MAS to Inverness, and how lack-lustre and lifeless the railway scene is becoming without the vitality of semaphore signalling. It also illustrates the effect that bi-directional signalling has in helping to achieve savings in the amount of infrastructure needed. This extends from Inverness station as far as the Cradlehall trailing and facing crossovers on the Aviemore Lines (roughly $1\frac{1}{2}$ miles away).

Plate 241
On 22nd August 1983, an immaculate Class 33/0 No. 33065 enters Redhill with the 7Y60 Departmental terminating working from
Tonbridge West Yard.

**The country end of Redhill station is a three-way split to Tonbridge (left), Brighton and Guildford. Viewed from platform 3, the bracket
signals are for the Down Through line (second from left), the lower arm applying to the Down Tonbridge line and the main arm reading
towards Brighton. The Platform line signals for the three routes were to the immediate left of the picture. In the distance is the SE
type timber Redhill "B" cabin, surrounded by its independent anti-bomb blast wall. It closed on 11th May 1985.**

Plate 242
Five years later, on 28th August 1988, a Class 119 dmu (cars 51079, 59437 and 51107) vacates platform 2 with the ECS from the 08.55 (SuO) from Tonbridge. This manoeuvre allowed the connecting Class 101 dmu on the 09.28 (SuO) Gatwick Airport to Reading service (in the far distance) to enter the same platform. The Airport dmus were introduced in 1980, to provide a faster link between Reading and Redhill than the through trains to Tonbridge. The Old Oak Common dmus first appeared on the line in 1979, when they gradually displaced BR(SR) demus including the famous Class 3-R "Tadpoles".

Here the track layout is very little changed from mechanical days. Consequently, the number of signalled routes from T485 (the Down Loop or Platform 3 signal with three-way theatre route indicator) and T487 (the Down Redhill signal with position 1 junction indicator) remains the same, although operated today from Three Bridges PSB. With Victoria PSB, it controls the whole of the Brighton line, working TCB to fringe boxes at London Bridge PSB, Oxted, Reigate, Tonbridge, Horsham, Lancing and Lewes. Seventy existing cabins were closed under this £120 million scheme. Note the new-style 25 mph circular retro- reflective (road traffic type) PSR sign, illustrating the principle of providing a theatre route indicator for a slow-speed route.

Plate 243
Both views on the Milford Haven branch were taken on 8th August 1988. This photograph shows Class 108 dmu Set S948 (cars 53928 and 51565) approaching Haverfordwest with the 09.34 Milford Haven to Swansea service.

We finish where we began, on the BR(WR), this time contrasting old and new equipment on a recent development: the resignalling of the Milford Haven branch, controlled from a new IFS panel in Clarbeston Road box. Completed on 11th September 1988, this scheme involved the closure of three ground frames at Herbrandston East and West Junctions, and Amoco Junction, and the cabins at Johnston and Haverfordwest, (see *SB*, Plate 337), with consequent track rationalisation. Viewed from the now bi-directionally signalled Up platform at Haverfordwest, the country end of the station presented an interesting scene of the unfolding transformation: No. 52 Down Loop to Down Main Starting signal (left); new 3-aspect colour light Down Platform signal CR17 (with St Andrew's cross hood, denoting it was then out of use); new 2-aspect colour light Up Platform (Down Direction) Starting signal, positioned in the formation of the former Up Loop; and bracket signal (right) with disused doll for No. 6 Up Main to Up Loop signal and No. 2 Up Main Home signal. To the left of the 30 mph PSR is a new barrow crossing Warning Indicator – a normally illuminated light, extinguished only on the approach of a train or during an electrical malfunction. This is an example of the fail-safe principle used extensively in railway signalling. The crossing should only be used by station staff when the indicator is lit.

Plate 244
Another Class 108 dmu, Set S949 (cars 53945 and 51563) negotiates Crundale Crossing with the 10.39 Swansea to Milford Haven train. (The external condition of the dmus is a credit to Landore depot.) With the exception of the summer Saturdays services for Tenby (1V31 from York and 1V42 from Leeds) and the return services (1E33 and 1E66 respectively), there are no regular locomotive hauled passenger services in West Wales.

The scheme also included the singling of the line between Johnston and Clarbeston Road, using the former Up line to Haverfordwest, and the former Down line thence to Clarbeston Road. In addition, Crundale Crossing, (see *SB*, Plate 103), on this latter section, was

converted to AHB. In this first stage of the work, while the Down Branch (right) was being refurbished, the crossing was in the throes of modernisation – note the concrete panels for the new single line, the level crossing gate, the old and new, bi-lingual notices, and the equipment room (right). The Up and Down Home semaphore signals had been abolished and the Up Branch was being used as the temporary single line, with Pilotman working in operation. No doubt Signalling Record Society members will recognise one of the Society's officers, John Morris, acting as pilotman on this occasion and sitting in the centre of the cab.

Index – Locations

Index – Locomotives & Multiple Units

Index – Signalling